Here's what the reviewers say about

I never promised you a Disneyland

"Jay Kesler has a way with words . . . and a way with kids. This is a book written for youth, but adults can profit from it. It's a call to a life of wholeness, to a realistic witness, and to a strong Christian faith in a non-Christian world. It's a book that speaks to needs. . . . "
—Denny Rydberg, Editor
The Wittenburg Door

"With a keen understanding of the questions that youth ask and the problems they face, and with a practical knowledge of the answers and solutions the Bible offers, Jay has come up with a great book to put into their hands. It is honest, practical, readable, and hammered out on the anvil of everyday experience."
—B. Clayton Bell, Pastor
Highland Park Presbyterian Church
Dallas, Texas

"If you are looking for something that speaks to young people where they are living, this is it. In an idiom that communicates, Jay Kesler shows how Christian faith meets head-on life's really big questions. He makes hackneyed truths become arrestingly fresh and relevant. . . . "
—Vernon G. Grounds, President
Conservative Baptist Theological Seminary

"Jay Kesler seems to scratch where youth itch—in language which makes sense. Many of the questions which so stubbornly pursue all of us will find satisfaction in this book."
—Richard C. Halverson, Pastor
Fourth Presbyterian Church
Washington, D.C.

I never promised you a Disneyland

by Jay Kesler
with Tim Stafford

Word Books, Publisher

Waco, Texas

I Never Promised You a Disneyland

Printed in the United States of America.
ISBN 0-87680-834-8
Library of Congress catalog card number: 75—10094

First paperback printing Sept. 1976

My thanks
to Tim Stafford
who recorded my ramblings
and put them in
intelligible form.
—Jay Kesler

Contents

Introduction

For many years the most likely place to find Jay
Kesler has been in the middle of a group of youth.
He's got medium height, sandy brown hair, and a
quick grin. He can be very, very funny: so funny he
has to restrain himself. He's spoken to thousands
of youth, filling the room with gestures, the black-
board with drawings, and the air with laughter. He
speaks and writes in ways people can understand.

But to really know him you have to see him after
he speaks. Surrounded by a group of kids with
questions and problems, he's relaxed. His mind
works quickly. He listens. He really hears the questions. He understands. He knows the problems
young Christians have: not only the angry questions
and the public questions, but those that come out
only after hours of talking one-to-one.

Jay Kesler also knows the answers. They aren't
pat answers, perhaps because he's lived the problems in his own life. He's tried the easy answers on
himself and knows they don't work. Instead, his
answers reach the deep questions in a way that
provides handles on life.

—TIM STAFFORD

1

what is God like?

(and how do I get in touch?)

Frank was a guy who really cared about life. He'd done lots of drugs but not for kicks. He was trying to get hold of life—trying to make sense of himself, the world, and God. When I talked to him I sensed that seriousness immediately. He listened very carefully.

"But Jay," he said, "I can't get hold of God. Every time I think I'm getting closer, I find out he isn't where I thought he was. It's like someone's taken an ice cream stick and scraped out his insides until there's just skin. But that's not right either. He doesn't even have a skin—at least not one I can touch."

I was tempted to pass it off as a cop-out, just another excuse for not accepting Christ. But I saw he was serious, and when I thought about what he was saying I realized it was a problem everyone

faces. Jesus recognized it, I think, when he told
Thomas, "You believe because you have seen me.
But blessed are those who haven't seen me and
believe anyway" (John 20:29).

That's the dilemma we have to face—under ordinary circumstances you don't see God. You don't
feel him. You don't audibly hear his voice. So when
you want to know him, get hold of him and understand him, you have a problem.

That's why there are so many misconceptions of
what God is and how to get to him. People always
have had these misconceptions. In the first century,
when Jesus lived, you might have had a very strange-
sounding idea of what God was like. In China or in
Rome, you might have thought he was the emperor.
If you wanted to get handles on God in Scandinavia
2,000 years ago, you put a maiden on a ship with
some fruits and vegetables, and sent her out to sea.
When the sea devoured her, you would think that
you had seen God at work. In Germany you might
have offered a young maiden, too—perhaps burned
her at the stake. In the British Isles you might have
participated in a cannibalistic ritual. On the Easter
Islands you might have carved a huge stone statue.

These may seem like ridiculous ways to get in
touch with God, but when you've posed the question, "How do you get in touch with God?" where
would you go to find a sensible answer? The only
way first-century man had was to look at the universe
God had made, and that universe was pretty harsh.

Therefore, men groping for God came up with a harsh projection of nature and called it God.

Technology has changed that by protecting us from cold, disease, starvation, and natural disasters that earlier men were constantly subjected to. Sometimes we end up with a smiling, bland, hand-holding God, just because that's the way the world around us seems.

But I'd still bet the average man, if he told you what he really thinks God is like, would come up with many of the ancient misconceptions. I think he'd say, for one thing, that God is harsh—that he's made up 10,000 sins that we can't avoid because of the natural desires and drives he's given us, and he's just waiting to catch us disobeying the rules so he can wipe us out. People still think God likes punishing people every chance he gets.

I suspect most people would also say that God is very distant. He's very high up in his heaven, and we're very small and insignificant—and that's the way God keeps it. If he'd let the sky crack at all so you could see him up there, he'd look like a combination of a lightning bolt and the Ajax man. Not the sort of God you'd want to get close to or talk to about your problems.

a surprising model

Jesus' disciples had similar ideas. True, they were Jewish, and so they had some good scriptural ideas of what God was like. But there were still problems for them. That's why they came to Jesus asking, "Lord, teach us how to pray." What they were really saying was, "How can we communicate with God? How can we understand him?" And Jesus answered in a startling way. He broke through many centuries of stiffness. He taught them to begin their prayers by addressing God, "Our Father." He didn't say, "Begin your prayers by saying 'Most High and Holy Potentate, Omnipotent and All-Powerful.' " He began the Lord's Prayer, a model for all other prayers, with one of the most ordinary, familiar words in existence, "Father."

God usually communicates to our world by taking things we know and relating them to greater things. Calling God "Father" is just one example. In other places in the Bible his love for us is compared to the love of an artist for an artifact, the love of a shepherd for his sheep, and a man's love for a woman. The chief Bible analogy, though, the one that Jesus chooses, is the idea of a father. We are the children; God is the father. What does this imply?

It means first of all, that God loves us. There is a kind of intimacy between parent and child that isn't in any other kind of relationship. (Unfortunately, all parents are less than perfect. This distorts what Jesus is saying a bit, for some people more than others.) This relationship is unique because it's one you don't have a choice in. You're born with parents; you don't get to pick and choose. Yet you're inextricably tied together. Few things can tear you up like a lousy relationship with parents. Few things can be

more deeply meaningful than a loving, growing relationship with them.

But that's a mere beginning image of the love we
can have with our heavenly Father, God. He is the
most loving, consistent Father possible. He looks
at us, always, with the tenderness a father feels
peeking into the cradle of his first baby.

But that's not all Jesus is implying. There's more
than tenderness in a father's love. A father wants
the very best for his children, and generally he can
see a little farther ahead than they can. That's why
all parents have rules.

crunched by a car

My children had a rule that they couldn't ride
their bikes in the street until they were eight years
old. All the other neighborhood kids were riding in
the street, but mine had to ride on the sidewalk.
They didn't like it. They thought I was really old-
fashioned, and when I told them I didn't want them
to get hit by a car, they didn't understand my rea-
soning. They'd complain, and I'm pretty sure they'd
sneak off on the street when I wasn't around. But
then one day Terry came home and said, "Timmy
got crunched by a car."

I said, "What do you mean, crunched by a car?"

She told me he'd been riding his bike in the street
and a car hit him. I said, "Now do you understand
why I don't want you to ride your bike in the street?"

"Yeah," she said. "You don't want me to get
crunched by a car."

I think that's the essence of the Ten Command-
ments. God doesn't say "Thou shalt not commit
adultery" and "Thou shalt not steal" because he's
trying to ruin our good times. He wants to protect
our happiness, not take it away. But when our happiness destroys other people's happiness, then God,
being the Father of the family, has to control it. He
does it with rules, like any father. The Ten Com-
mandments are like stop signs. They're not there
to wreck our transmission or to increase our driving
time. They're sort of an agreement: I'll stop, and
you'll stop, and that way we don't kill each other.

This is why God isn't just all warm and fuzzy feelings. Sometimes he seems to bristle with rules. But
they're rules with a purpose, because God, much
more than our human fathers, really knows what's
going on. He sees the future. He knows precisely
the kind of person you are. He knows what things
are really important in life.

There's one more aspect of fatherhood that probably wouldn't occur to you because our society is
different from Jesus'. Jesus came from a strong
Jewish family, and for the Jews the father was
always—for all of life—the most important person.
You didn't get away from him just by going away
to college. In all probability you lived in the same
house with him all your life. The oldest man in the
family always spoke first. There was deep respect
and reverence for him.

The same thing is true of God. You don't lightly
call him by his first name. You don't kick him out

of the house when you're tired of him. You can never really leave him behind when you go away to college or get married. He's always there and always demands to be treated with great respect and reverence. He's not your buddy; he's your Father—your link with all the wisdom and understanding there is in the universe.

One other thing about fathers ties into this. Because your father isn't your buddy (or at least wasn't in a Jewish home), you might not go to him for every little problem. But when you run up against problems you can't solve yourself, you want to talk to someone with a little more ability to help—someone with enough experience and power to understand. You go to your father. That is the way God is with us. Let's face it, there are problems we can hassle out ourselves. But when things are really on the edge of despair, we need a Father in heaven who is ready to listen and help.

a blimp

Imagine a blimp tied up at an airport. Untied, the blimp just blows back and forth, without any control. It needs firm mooring lines to hold it firmly in place so it'll still be flying high the next morning. Lacking them, it may fly high for a while, but it will also lose control and crash.

Faith in Christ is like that. You can directly, emotionally, experience God's goodness to you, but that alone is like the blimp without moorings. That's why people who never get into the Word of God often

drift from drugs to the occult to Christianity to East-
ern religions. They're flying high, but without controls they crash.

God doesn't have a skin. He doesn't give us something tangible we can physically hold onto. But he
does give us, through the Bible and through Jesus,
some moorings. They're things that don't change—
truths that we can grab onto and hold no matter how
we're feeling. One is this truth—God is our Father.
It'll help hold you steady while you soar.

2

why did Jesus come?

The greatest contact of all time between God and us came when Jesus Christ, God's son, came to earth. We celebrate his birth at Christmas. Most people, when they think of Christmas, think of camels, swaddling clothes, and a manger. But I think of a Ford Motor plant.

One year I toured a plant and watched them assemble cars. It was an eye-opener. I'd always had the idea Ford would just guess how many cars they needed, and make that many. They'd decide to make green cars one day, and make two or three thousand. Then they'd switch to some other color.

But of course, that's not the way they do it. All over America people walk into Ford dealerships, look around, kick a few tires, and then order a car—a certain model with specific equipment, color, roof, transmission, and defroster. The dealer fills out a computer card and an order is placed with Ford. In one city they make the correct transmission, and in another city they make vinyl roofs, and in another

19

mirrors. All these places start feeding their products toward the Ford plant.

The Ford plant has a man who puts on steering wheels. The cars come down the line, and when the green cars come you can bet he doesn't get a red steering wheel to put on. At exactly the right time, the green steering wheels are there. He reaches out, grabs one, and sticks it on. That's what happens with each part—the mirror, the roof, the seat covers —every part shows up at precisely the right instant.

Now if man is capable of designing such an ingenious system to bring thousands of events and people together with precision timing just to make a car, imagine what God can do in preparing for his visit to earth. That's what I think of at Christmas— the number of things God brought together at one time in one place is so incredible, it makes the Ford plant look like the corner gas station.

the scheme of things

Some people have the idea that Jesus was a remedial action, a sort of last minute Band-Aid stuck on a wounded world. God had tried everything else, so he decided to try his Son. But the Bible says Jesus came in the fullness of time—when everything was as fully prepared for him as possible. All the pieces of history fell together.

The preparation God did is staggering. God had used a man named Alexander to conquer the entire known world and spread Greek as a language for practically every educated person. The good news about Jesus Christ could spread without language barriers because of that.

Then there was the Roman Empire—a government that just happened to build good roads throughout the known world so that travel was easy —again, providing an easier way for the gospel to spread. And think of the thousands of years God had worked with the Jewish people, opening up their understanding of him so they were ready for the things Jesus said and did.

God had spent thousands of years getting ready to come! All his preparation culminated in a single, incongruous event—a baby born to noninfluential people in a rural town of a small, conquered nation. The only fanfare for the greatest event in history was heard by a bunch of no-account shepherds.

Jesus was no Ajax man

Now, what do you make of that? All that preparation and no publicity at the actual event. Isn't that like preparing a senior banquet for months and then forgetting to send out invitations?

Not if you see the point. The wise men, the shepherds, the manger—those weren't just thrown into the story for local color. They hint at other fantastic things about how God treats the world . . . things you might never guess.

When people through the ages have thought about how God might come to earth, most of the time they've thought of him coming down in a chariot of fire to do some fantastic thing—kind of a religious

Ajax man. You find this idea in most of the early religions—the Roman and Greek and Phoenician mythologies.

But Mary and Joseph were just poor young people. A carpenter then was probably about as prestigious as a carpenter now. Christmas makes the point that God deliberately sent his Son to the humblest of people. By sending his Son to people like that, God was telling us he isn't concerned about how much money you make or how many people know your name. No matter how unimportant everybody else thinks you are, he doesn't think so. It was your kind of people that he chose as parents for his Son. Not only was he willing to visit them, he was willing to become one of them. Jesus came as a human baby. He didn't suddenly appear in shining armor.

This is hard to grasp. God became man! Jesus was one of us! He went through the same kinds of problems we go through. The Bible says he was tempted in every way we're tempted. That means, for instance, he must have been sexually tempted. He had to work at controlling his impulses just as we do. If he didn't, then Jesus was hollow. He looked like a man on the outside, but if he wasn't really tempted, his insides were empty of the problems we face.

But Jesus wasn't a hollow man. He gave up his privileges as God and became a man. He was living proof that you don't have to be superhuman to live the kind of life you were meant to. You just have to be obedient to God.

Sometimes I wish I could solve all my problems by magic, just whisk them away. But Jesus didn't handle his own troubles that way. He faced them. So I know I'm going to have to face them in the same way. What's more, I know it's possible to face them with Jesus and come out on top. Because Jesus stayed perfect using the same weapons I have at my disposal.

moving up alongside the world

God came to earth as a man so we'd have a realistic model to follow. But there's another reason. To saddle a horse, you put your hand on him slowly and move it gently up his side. Gradually you move up alongside him so that he's used to you, and then you put the saddle on. That way you don't spook the horse.

In a sense that's what God was doing in Bethlehem. He was moving up the side of mankind slowly so we wouldn't get all tense. He wanted to do some things that wouldn't be possible from a fiery chariot. God wanted to identify with man, not give him advice. If he'd wanted to give advice, he could have done it with a bullhorn from heaven. Instead he came as a child. Even the most timid person isn't afraid of an infant.

Even when Jesus did exciting things, they didn't necessarily seem exciting. Jesus was moving up slowly. If you look back at the events in the New Testament you say, Wow! and try to synthetically reproduce the excitement in your own life. If you do, you'll be frustrated. Take the Christmas scene for instance. Spectacular? As far as everybody in town was concerned, nothing was happening. People were standing in line to make out their tax returns, pushing and shoving. Everybody was trying to find a place to stay for the night, and one unfortunate young couple couldn't squeeze in. The guy in charge of the local hotel generously tried to provide a place by clearing out a stable, and Joseph saw it was better than sleeping outside, so he took it. Sure a baby was born there, but in those days, where were most of the babies born? People were having them in tents out in the desert. It probably wasn't too unusual. As far as everybody around was concerned, that was a ho-hum night.

That's the way God's working now. There are lots of things around that appear ho-hum, but are really very spectacular if you dig deep. Answered prayer for instance. Sometimes when God answers I'm prompted to say, "Big deal. Maybe it was a coincidence." Or somebody becoming a Christian. To the neighborhood maybe it isn't even worth yawning about. But to those inside, with eyes to see, it's the greatest miracle of all.

the original pattern

We are to imitate Jesus in our lives. He is the pattern we are to live by. But we need to make sure we're dealing with the real pattern, not some feeling we've built up. What really happened back then? If we know that, then we can act consistently with it.

My dad tells a story about raising a barn for a man whose barn had burned. All the people in the neighborhood came together and assigned certain guys to cut the rafters. All these guys had to do was follow a pattern.

But instead of using the original pattern for each rafter that was to be cut, they would mark one, cut it, and then use it to mark the next one, and so on. Each time they marked a rafter, however, they were gaining just one pencil width in length. Each marking would only add 1/32 of an inch or so at each end. It doesn't amount to much, except they kept compounding it until they were one-half inch off on the sixteenth rafter. By the thirty-second rafter they were one inch off its pattern. Eventually they realized their error, and had to recut all the rafters.

Some of us are in that position when it comes to following Jesus—we're copying something somebody told us or some feeling we remember, and we're missing the mark.

This is why the Bible goes to such pains to tell us what Jesus was really like. He is the pattern we're supposed to live by. The person who wants to follow Christ has to keep going back to that original pattern.

I particularly stress the Bible, God's Word. The psalmist wrote, "How can a young man stay pure? By reading your Word and following its rules. I have thought much about your words, and stored them in my heart so that they would hold me back from sin" (Ps. 119: 9, 11). There are certain habits of Bible study and prayer which lead you back to the original pattern of Jesus Christ. I put a high priority on developing those habits. I've learned not to make all kinds of lofty ideals for myself, but to think of practical vows like, "I will not go to bed at night without reading from the Bible." A morning person might say, "I won't start the day without Bible reading and prayer."

Here's a formula that's helped me. I begin by bowing and acknowledging God and his control of my life, and ask him to teach me one specific thing from his Word. Then as soon as something specific jumps out, and the Spirit seems to underline it in my mind, I stop right there and meditate on it. I ask God to add that particular virtue to my life.

That doesn't sound like much—but suppose I learned one lesson a day. That would be 365 lessons in a year. In ten years it would be over 3,650. That would be quite a few lessons to learn from the original pattern.

So Christmas is more than a fun celebration. It's the beginning of a God-man pattern for us to follow. If we can see the incredible richness of his story, it'll give those Christmas carols, gifts, and warm feelings a lot more meaning. Because Christ came to earth, you can never realistically think that God can't help you with your problems. He can, because he's been where you are.

3

in touch with God

He came up to me after I was finished speaking with that look of sublime certainty in his eye. He didn't think I was very spiritual. He was hoping to help me out.

So I said, "Will you pray for me?" and I bowed my head. He was taken aback a little, but he did, and I thanked him. Then I began to probe him a little on what his idea of spirituality was. Soon it was obvious that my idea of spirituality was a little different from his. I was asking, "Besides praying that the Holy Spirit will bless us by giving warm feelings and cozy groups to share in, isn't it spiritual to pray that he'll show us down-and-out people we can help? Is there a widow on your block whose lawn you could mow? Are there lonely people at school you could be a friend to? Does your church have missionaries over-seas that you could concentrate on praying for? Are you using your money to help anybody?"

And he didn't really think of those things as "spir-itual."

Just what does it mean to be spiritual? The first definition that comes to mind might be something like, "being in touch with God." But how do you measure that? By good feelings? By the number of people you've witnessed to? How does a person go about being "in touch with God?"

One very popular definition today seems to be "the more removed from the world you are, the more your mind is constantly on spiritual things, the more spiritual you are." Translated into the way other people see Christians it means, "the more weird you are, the better Christian you must be." It's this kind of definition that brought the sentence, "He's so heavenly minded he's no earthly good."

This kind of spirituality only cares about souls. It makes the earth just one big train station: a place where people decide whether they'll get on the train bound for heaven or not; a place to be escaped as soon as possible. You shouldn't use your mind: that's no use to God. The only thing you should read is the Bible. There's a commune in California where they practice this: only the leader can read anything besides the Bible. He reads the newspaper each day so he can report to the group on what Bible prophecies were fulfilled.

Sports, of course, are pointless. So are art, beauty, ecology, politics, you name it. Why should we pay attention to them? The whole point of life is to get off the earth, away from these minds that hang us up with constant questions and doubts, away from these bodies that are always making us lustful or sleepy when we're praying.

Most Christians go through a stage where they believe this. I did. It's popular because most of us don't like life too well. The world is a confusing, demanding, difficult place to live in. It's hostile. We want to put signs on it that read, "Danger, Keep Away."

was Jesus spiritual?

But when you read the Bible, you have a hard time holding that view. Jesus was criticized for going to too many parties with the wrong kind of people. When he prayed his last prayer for the disciples in John 17 he specifically said, "I do not ask you to take them out of the world."

And if the world is just something we're trying to get away from, why did God look at it after he'd made it and say, "It is very good"?

Besides that, I don't think God is inefficient. If all he cared about were our souls, it'd be much simpler to make us fuzzy gray balls floating in space. No minds, no real bodies, no personalities—just "souls." Why go to the trouble of making us so complicated?

True spirituality is bigger than just souls, praying, and Bible reading. But how can we define it?

The definition of spirituality I support came to me years ago when I was asking a different kind of question. That was in the early days of Youth for Christ.

What hit us then was the fact that people between the ages of thirteen and nineteen are in a very special position. They're adults in many ways, and yet

they're still living under other people's authority—
their parents, teachers, coaches, and bosses. What
does the Bible have to say to their situation?

Really, it doesn't say much. Mostly it deals with
men and women who are fully adults. You do have
Mary pregnant at thirteen or fourteen, but in their
society she was considered fully mature, ready for
the responsibility of being an adult.

Then we noticed this statement in Luke 2:52
about Jesus' boyhood: "And Jesus kept increasing
in wisdom and stature, and in favor with God and
men."

That statement contains everything we know
about Jesus between the time he turned twelve and
his baptism by John the Baptist at the age of thirty.
Considering the kind of person Jesus turned out to
be, those years of development must have been on
target. Maybe, we thought, this would give some
clues to a young person's spirituality.

So we looked more carefully at that verse to see
the various components. First, we noticed Jesus
grew in wisdom—that's the sphere of the mind. He
also grew in stature—in other words, his body was
growing. He grew in favor with God—the spiritual
dimension was well adjusted.

He got along with his peers. We looked at these
four areas—mental, physical, spiritual, and social—
and saw that they were all important. It wasn't
enough to grow only in relationship to God—you
also had to grow in relationship to your friends. You
had to grow physically and mentally. Why? Because
Jesus did.

Later I noticed a similarity in another crucial passage, Romans 12:1–2. Paul writes, "I beg you, my brothers, as an act of intelligent worship, to give him your bodies [physical] as a living sacrifice, consecrated by him and acceptable to him. Don't let the world around you squeeze you into its own mold [social], but let God remold your minds [mental] from within, so that you may prove in practice that the plan of God for you is good [spiritual]." Once again, there were four general areas that seemed important.

From this came the concept of the balanced life. Remembering these four areas, we said, helps you keep a healthy perspective on yourself. Everyone will probably emphasize one of these areas more than the others: an athlete will emphasize the physical, a genius will emphasize the mental. But if you remember that all of these areas should show development, then you will be a balanced, healthy person. That's why we still refer today in **Campus Life** to the "balanced life." We don't think any of these areas should be left out.

was Beethoven balanced?

I've had kids come up to me and say, "Was Beethoven balanced? Seems to me that the people who really accomplish great things are imbalanced, they're driven in one direction. What you're saying seems to make everyone normal, healthy, and bland."

And I can't deny that a lot of the greatest men and women of history were not normal, but eccentric. A lot of them weren't easy to get along with. They had such deep interests in one area that they couldn't pay attention to anything else.

But I wonder what made them eccentric. Were they eccentric because they chose to be? Did Beethoven choose to suffer emotionally? Or was he forced into that role by people who couldn't take what he was doing and saying? A lot of the great writers and musicians say things so true that people can't listen to them. But the great artist has to tell the truth; he can't compromise it. So he ends up driven by other people into eccentricity. He didn't necessarily have to be that way to be creative.

And let's make a distinction here. There are lots of "driven" men around. There are devils that want to "drive" you to some cause or another. But some great men, like Gandhi or Martin Luther King, were driven by truly great compassion and ideals. Others, like Hitler, were driven by hatred and a lust for power. There's nothing great about being driven. It all depends on what you're driven by.

You could say Jesus Christ was as eccentric as any man who lived. Why couldn't he forget his obsession about God? Why not settle down in Nazareth, get married, and "cool it"? He couldn't, because he was driven too: driven by the love of God and the desire to do his will. So when the Spirit led Jesus into his public ministry, he responded. There was no compromise. But that didn't make him "imbalanced" in the sense I mean here. Since God wanted Jesus to serve him in that unique way, it was the only way he could be truly balanced. He didn't neglect the physical, the social, or the mental areas of life. He had friends. He was no anti-intellectual. He wasn't a weakling. But he followed the will of God. He was driven, but driven by the Holy Spirit. That kind of "drivenness" never becomes imbalanced.

To the world, Jesus did everything wrong. He didn't run over his adversaries; in fact, he said "love your enemies." He was nonviolent. He didn't publicize himself. When he did something stupendous, most of the time he'd tell the witnesses not to tell anyone.

The Roman Empire was hardly an age for becoming famous that way. The Empire was the age of the conquering Caesars. But how many of those fierce conquering Caesars can you name? They're just half-forgotten names attached to a bronze helmet in a history book. Jesus, the insignificant, unpublicized, itinerant preacher, is certainly the most famous man who ever lived.

true spirituality

So far, I've mentioned the spiritual as though it were one-fourth of a balanced life, sort of a separate holy little room in your insides.

But that isn't an accurate picture either.

The real truth is more startling, more removed from the stereotyped "religious" answer. The "spiritual" dimension is the point at which all the other dimensions of life—the mental, physical, and social—are committed to God. There is **no** spiritual dimension to life where there isn't a mental, physical, or social dimension. Spirituality doesn't happen in a vacuum.

This is where commitment takes on real meaning. When someone becomes a Christian we say he "commits himself to Christ." But what does that mean? Does it imply a little ceremony in church where you stand up and walk down the aisle? Does it only imply that you pray certain words?

No, it means the commitment of each area of life to God. God wants us, Paul says in Romans 12, to present our bodies as a living sacrifice to him. The emphasis is on the **living.** He isn't interested in human sacrifice, as so many pagan religions have thought. He wants living sacrifices: people who eat, play, talk, think, and make friends in a way that is consciously committed to God. That's what true spirituality is about.

The devil also wants a living sacrifice. He wants **you to be** irresponsible in the way you act. He wants you to eat, play, talk, think, and make friends **his** way. So there is a constant battle going on over you. And you're the one who makes the decisions.

God wants you to commit your body to him. That means, first of all, that you shouldn't abuse your body. Smoking is a lousy idea. Being out of shape is a bad idea. Drugs or drunkenness are bad ideas. Why? Because they're not responsible uses of your body. They're not wrong because God drew up an arbitrary list of things he wanted to deprive us of.

They're wrong because they're against the positive act of committing your body to Christ.

Do you realize that playing sports can be a spiritual exercise? It can be, because God is interested in your body. Are you staying in shape? Do you get enough sleep, eat the right food, keep your weight down? Those are spiritual battles. The devil wants you to be irresponsible. God wants you to be responsible!

It goes farther than that. You can misuse your body subtly. A girl can use her body irresponsibly with guys. She can use it to manipulate them. Certain girls can lead a boy around by the nose with their bodies. That's not a responsible use of the girl's body, because it denies the boy (and the girl) full personhood.

A fellow can get infatuated with his body. He can care for nothing except how tremendous an athlete he is. He can groom his body as though there were no tomorrow. But that would be irresponsible, too—not because being a good athlete is wrong, but because God made us more than bodies. Athletics isn't an end in itself.

How about your minds? I'd say the biggest lack of spirituality in the realm of the mind stems from laziness. People don't use their minds fully. For some reason Christians are often more guilty of this than other people, as though being ignorant were somehow spiritual. I look around a room of Christian kids and I wonder, "Could there be a cure for cancer in this room? Could there be a great piece of music?

Could there be a novel as great as **War and Peace?**

But it won't happen if you don't give your mind to God. Where do you think Jonas Salk, who dis-covered the vaccine for polio, would be if he had had your attitude in chemistry?

And what are you letting your mind soak up? Is it soaking up a lot of quiz shows, or pornography? Or is it becoming saturated with the Word of God?

There are whole other areas of the mind to give to God. How about your thoughts about the opposite sex? Do you think of people selfishly, in terms of what they have to offer you? Or do your thoughts center on how you can responsibly show love to them?

Of course, this spills over into the whole area of relationships. These need to be given to God, too. You should commit your friendships to the kind of relationship that can really reflect God's love. And you shouldn't only include the beautiful people in your friendships. All people are God's children, whether they're lovely to look at or not.

But this area can be subtle, too. Suppose you have a close group of friends. You value the fact that these friends think highly of you. You value the closeness.

Then suppose someone new starts hanging around the fringe of the group. How do you react? If you're irresponsible, you start thinking how you can protect your status and position in the group. You worry about losing the closeness of your little group.

But if you commit your social life to God, then you welcome this person. You trust God to take care of your need of friendship. You look for opportunities to befriend anyone.

These kinds of commitments—physical, mental, and social—go on and on. There isn't any end. The more you experience life, the more you grow as a Christian, the more you see areas of life you need to give to God. Things you wouldn't have thought had anything to do with God become great areas to grow in spiritually.

Suppose you reach eighty or ninety years of age. By this time you've given just about everything in your life to God. There are very few things your commitment to Christ doesn't cover.

Imagine old Fred, eighty-five, riding along in his car with his wife Maude. In front of him there are two teenagers snuggled up to one another. The girl is nibbling the guy's ear and he's got his arm around her. Old Fred gets all worked up. He turns to his wife Maude and says, "Maude, just look at those disgusting kids. Kids just aren't like we were. They have smutty minds. Why aren't they interested in doing things like we did when we were young, like going to church every night of the week, listening to two-hour sermons, and praying for three hours at a time? It's disgusting!"

But Maude leans over and says kind of sweetly, "Fred, remember when we were going together that time we parked out by the cemetery . . . ?"

"I don't remember anything of the kind!" Fred exclaims, and he drives grumpily along muttering about how the kids are going to the dogs.

That night old Fred doesn't sleep too well, and he lies in bed thinking about those kids, and he realizes he was wrong. So he prays, "God, I'm sorry I judged those kids. Help me to mind my own business and to have an open mind about things." Then he turns over and goes to sleep. It's really beautiful, because Fred, at eighty-five, has found yet another area of life he can give to God.

This is what spirituality is all about: a **living** sacrifice to God. It's life committed to God. It's **life** aware that God is involved, that he is offering his grace and forgiveness.

And it keeps going and growing. It doesn't wear out, where that narrow box of "spirituality" divorced from everything else soon becomes irrelevant, just a habit or an emotional release you use occasionally. Real spirituality goes on forever.

4

I can't stand myself

George was a terrific person. He could tell jokes that made everybody laugh, he was pretty good at sports, and people naturally liked him. In fact, everybody liked George except George. I know, because I talked to him a lot, and when you really got under the surface you could tell. He was full of self-doubt. He hated looking in the mirror.

How come? George had a nose on his face that looked like Jimmy Durante's after vitamins. You wouldn't necessarily call it ugly—but you would certainly call it big. And when George thought about himself, he thought about that nose. He didn't think about all his good qualities. He thought of that big, ugly (in his eyes) schnozzle.

He's not alone. If God advertised that he'd do alterations at such and such a place, the line would be endless. Just about everyone has something he doesn't like about himself: pimples, shyness, big mouth, too tall, short, fat, skinny, curly hair, straight hair, lack of athletic ability.

39

It's obviously not good for people to dislike themselves. It's depressing to them, and what's more, it insults God. They didn't make themselves; God made them. When someone looks in the mirror and makes a face, he's making a face at God.

But knowing that doesn't necessarily help. The feelings are still there. What can you do?

vive la difference

The first thing is to understand why God made you the way he did. Why did God make tall people and short people, thin people and wide people, active people and slow people, talkative people and quiet people? Why did God make big noses?

The Scriptures say that when God looked at the world he'd made, he said it was good. He didn't say, "The handsome things are good." All of it was good! If you forget yourself for a while, you see this is true. Differences are what make people interesting. What would Barbra Streisand be without that nose? Vive la difference!

Then look at a magazine like **Vogue,** where every picture fits someone's ideal standards of beauty. What's the result? A plastic sameness that makes it impossible to even remember the girls' faces. When everyone's the same, that means everyone gets lost.

God could have made people like Henry Ford made cars: every one the same. It probably would have been more efficient, and certainly no one would have complained that he got a bad deal. But God did exactly the opposite. How many variables are there? Noses, mouths, eyes, ears, skin, height, weight and a few more. But in the same way the telephone company takes seven digits and makes a different combination for everybody, God uses those differences to make us so that, really, there are no two people on earth exactly alike.

Maybe you've never thought about why God did that. It's easy to take it for granted. But it means something. The medium is the message, and the message is, God loves variety. He made us different because he thought we deserved to be different. He doesn't work only with masses of people, like a statistical sociologist. He works with individuals. He likes individuality.

Who are you to say God made a mistake when he made you? What makes you think God blew it when he didn't make you the All-American Everything? God thinks you're something special, and he wants you to think the same.

spiritual Kamikaze

Some people will tell you the Bible says just the opposite. They look at Galatians 2:20, "I have been crucified with Christ: and I myself no longer live, but Christ lives in me." They think that means spiritual Kamikaze. They figure the best Christians are those who crawl out from between the mattress and the springs and say, "I'm nothing. I'm a worm. I can't do it. Whatever it is you want, I can't do it." They go for annihilating self-respect, and whenever they feel proud of something they were part of, they have to hide that feeling.

Trouble is, it's phony. No matter how hard they try, these people aren't genuinely humble. They put it on. They're just trying to look good in another way. "I bet I'm twice as humble as you are."

Scripture says the humble man is the honest man. You're not supposed to think of yourself more highly than you deserve. And you're to think of others before yourself. But that doesn't mean you make yourself into a worm. You're not a worm! If God wanted you to be a worm, he wouldn't have had any trouble making you one. He's very good at worms.

This worm theology creates a lot of problems. A person who can't accept himself generally has trouble relating to others. Jesus said we should love our neighbor as we love ourselves—and if we don't love ourselves, where does that leave our neighbor?

There are, of course, some problems to loving yourself. Most of us aren't too lovable. We have some lovable qualities, but lots of unlovable ones, too. If we try seriously to love ourselves as Christ wants us to, we run into problems. There are things in us that make complete love impossible.

Jesus changes all this. When we accept his forgiveness he wipes out our sin, so we're not only acceptable to him, though that is the main thing, but so we're acceptable to ourselves. God has made us whole again, and no matter how many times we mess up our lives, he continues to renew us. Because of that, we can love ourselves. We can begin to really love others.

The worm theology isn't all wrong, of course. There **is** something potentially bad about loving yourself. It's selfishness. It's the idea that the whole world should be tailored to your liking.

But that doesn't mean the self is out of the picture. You aren't to destroy that, you're to use it to serve God.

Every attribute has two sides. Take the word "child." If someone is childish, that's a bad thing. But if he or she is child-like, that's good. There isn't a word "self-like," but there is a word "selfish." Selfishness is absolutely wrong. It's the corruption of the virtue of loving yourself, a virtue God wants for each of us.

computer-designed tire

There's a commercial on TV that says a certain kind of tire has a "computer-designed tread." It makes me mad every time I see it. No computer ever designed a tread. Some very smart men used a computer as a tool when they were designing the tread of the tire. So why don't they say that? Why not say, "Designed by some of the smartest men in the world"? Simply because people are constantly putting down the whole human race. Half the world believes a computer is actually smarter than a man, which is total nonsense.

But you don't get that impression from our society. You watch TV and find out you're not as smart as a computer. You pick up a magazine and realize your body doesn't make the **Vogue** or **Sports Illustrated** standard. You go to school and find out you're not good enough to make the most popular crowd. It's interesting, in some ways the world's standards are much harder to meet than Jesus' standards of acceptance. You never really make the world's standards. There's always one more rung on the ladder of success. But you're already accepted by Jesus no matter who you are.

So the Christian really must have a different standard. If you take your temperature with a thermometer that's out of kilter, you may find out you have the world's worst temperature. That's why getting rid of the world's thermometer—the standards set by the world and the kids at school—and measuring yourself by God's standards is essential. God's standard is that a man is successful not by his appearance or his ability, but by what is in his heart.

This is where your personal time with God and his Word are essential. As you read the Bible you find repeatedly that God's standards are stressed. You learn to live by them because you're saturated with an understanding of them every day. Then when you pray you thank God for what he's done— including making you the way you are, and making your world the way it is. You realize as you pray and meditate that God cares about you—the unique, invaluable **you.**

you're okay

But it isn't the sort of thing you can do alone. You need help from other Christians, too. Christians should be bearing each other's burdens; loving each other; pointing out each other's good qualities.

This can really help. It reinforces God's standards of measurement in our lives. And it helps us feel better about ourselves.

Why not try an experiment? Instead of always complaining to each other about how our lives aren't all they could be, how about building each other up? Why not make a point of telling your Christian friends what you find great about them? They are, Scripture says, gifts of God to you. Let them know that by the standards of Christ they are tremendous people. You may find that when you help them believe in themselves, their performance as Christians improves.

the rose garden

I once had a very flowery way of talking about this. I would talk about man as the pinnacle of God's creation, and I'd illustrate it with the idea of the plant world as a pyramid. At the bottom are the algae and the lichens, up a little further are the weeds and grasses, and at the top you find the crowning achievement: the rose. It's very fragile, beautiful, and complex. All the other plants are great, but the rose is something very, very special.

Now man, I said, is also at the top of a pyramid, but this pyramid isn't just plants or animals. It's the whole universe. Man, I said, is the finest thing God has made. We're like the rose—the very top. God cared so much about us he sent his son to die for us.

Then once this old guy came up after I was done. He was very polite. "How much do you know about roses?" he asked.

I said I didn't know too much, really.

"Well," he said, "I do." He'd been raising prize-winning roses for years and years. "You know," he said, "if you leave a rose just as God created it, it's a pretty small thing. You get a little flower and a lot of thorns. But when man cooperates with God, as rose-fanciers do, then you really get something. You get the roses that people really love, in all their wild variation of color and beauty."

He was saying there's more to life than accepting the fact that God made us and thinks we're pretty tremendous. That's important—very important. But if you start with self-acceptance, you have to move on to self-improvement. God loves you exactly the way you are, but there are some things he would like to see you change. When you work with him at changing them you become more than a wild rose— you become a really beautiful, cultured rose.

I once met a girl who had this problem. She was tremendously overweight. She wanted to talk to me and I hardly had to say a word. Her story just came pouring out, problem after problem. Her pastor couldn't help her; he just got nervous when she came around. Her folks didn't love her and were always picking on her. Teachers made fun of her right in front of other kids at school. It was just an awful world. She showed me a scar on her forehead where her dad had hit her once—he was always hitting her.

This went on for an hour, nonstop. I just sat there listening, feeling for her, trying to empathize with her problems. But it got a little thick. You know how it is when somebody is so picked on you wonder if he doesn't deserve it.

Finally after an hour I stopped her and said something that I would never normally say to someone I didn't know well. "Elaine," I said, "how many of your problems are directly related to the fact that you're about a hundred pounds overweight?"

She stopped cold. She sat stunned for a moment, and then she started to cry. She cried and cried, and I began to wonder if I should have said it. She paused for a second and looked up at me and whimpered, "You know, nobody ever said anything like that to me before."

"Well, you still haven't answered my question," I said. "How many of your problems are directly related to your weight?"

She cried a little more, and then she said, "I guess about all of them."

"Well, then what are we going to do about it? Do you think I ought to give you a Bible verse to read? Or sit you under a tree to meditate? Have a word of prayer about it? What's going to solve this problem?

"I'm not a medical doctor," I said. "I don't know a thing about medicine. But I'd suggest you go to a doctor and get a diet. And then you stick to it."

Then I added, "There is one thing I can do to help. I can be your friend. You can write to me and tell me how you're doing, and I'll write and encourage you along."

So for three years she wrote me every week. "Lost a pound." "Gained two." "Lost five." "Gained three." Slowly, painfully, she made progress. When she was a senior in high school, she sent me her school paper. It had her picture on the front page. We're not talking about Cinderella here: she was still what you would call plump. She'd won some kind of academic award, and that's why her picture was in the paper. But it said, "I'm somebody." Before, she'd been nobody.

Along with the picture was a letter that said, "Jay, I don't think I'll be writing you any more. It's not that I don't like you. It's just that I realize I've needed you as a sort of crutch to build me up, and now I don't think I'll be needing that. So thanks very much."

The key turning point had come about six months after we started on the project. She wrote me a letter, and she said, "Jay, I've been lying to you. My dad isn't really that bad a person. Neither is my pastor or the kids at school. The truth is, I hated myself so badly that I found myself blaming these other people."

That's typical of all of us. What we can't stand in ourselves we put on other people. If you feel like that, there are two messages God has for you. They're the same things Elaine had to learn. The first is that God loves you, no matter who you are. His standards are a lot different from the world's. If you're not quite like everybody else it's because he didn't want you like everybody else.

The other thing is that if your problems are something you can solve, as Elaine's were, then God wants to lovingly and firmly help you solve them. It isn't that he'll love you more then. He already loves you more than you can imagine, just as you are. But because he loves you, he wants you to be all you can be.

5

pressure

It was dark. All the meetings were over, and I was walking along past the camp dining hall. There was a huge pile of firewood stacked beside it, lumpy, dark, and ominous. From behind it came a hoarse, whispering voice.

"Hey, Jay."

I peered into the darkness and made out the figure of a boy I'd seen a lot of that week.

"C'mere a minute," he said.

His name was Neal, about seventeen years old, built like a Greek god. He'd won everything that week—softball, basketball, swimming. He was a fantastic athlete, and seemed to have his head on straight, too. He sat in the front row at every meeting, answered all the questions, volunteered for everything. All the girls thought he was great.

"What's the matter?" I asked, standing with him behind the woodpile.

"I'm worried about what happens when I go home from camp tomorrow," he said.

51

"What for?" I asked.

"Well, I've been through this before," he said. "Within the week I'll be acting just like I was before —it happens every year. When I'm up here with Christian kids, I completely absorb their way of life. I know all the songs, I know all about the Bible, I act like they do. And it's not a put-on either, Jay. I really enjoy myself. But at home with my buddies, it's different. I do just as good a job absorbing their environment as I do with Christian kids. I talk bad; I booze it up; I chase after girls—just the opposite of how I am here."

He was staring down at his feet as he was talking. "In fact, Jay, the best way to understand me is this: I'm a chameleon. Whatever color you put me down on, that's the color I turn. I have no character of my own. I just pick up whatever I'm around."

I thought about chameleons. In the third grade, chameleons were the big thing in South Bend, Indiana. There was a five-and-dime store near our house, and in the back they had a pet section with fish, turtles, hamsters, mice, and chameleons. On the way to school we'd buy a chameleon. They'd put it in an ice cream container for us to carry, and when we got outside we'd stuff it in our pockets. If anyone asked us why we had it, we said, "Science." That shut them up.

When things got dull at school, we'd take out our chameleons. They were fun to play with. You could always scare the girls with them. But the neatest thing was watching them change color. For some reason, if you put the chameleon on a book it would change its color to the book's. Put it half on the geography book and half on the math book, and it'd be half green and half brown.

It seemed great to be a chameleon—you could be any color you wanted. But from the chameleon's point of view, it wasn't necessarily so great. If a chameleon decided he wanted to be gray, and then somebody put him on a green book, he turned green —whether he wanted to or not. He was a pawn to his environment, and it could be very frustrating to him.

While I was thinking about this, Neal was waiting to hear what I would have to say. "Look, Neal," I said, "I think you need to have some real freedom in your life."

"Freedom?" he said. "I've got too much freedom —so much freedom, all I ever do is get into trouble."

"But real freedom isn't the lack of external controls," I said. "Real freedom is being able to choose your own response to any situation. If he's with people who are laughing, a free person should be able to be sober if he wants to. If he's with gossiping people, he should be able to keep quiet if he wants. He ought to be able to choose what he wants to be, not merely absorb his environment."

I began to tell him the difference between how God and Satan treat you. Read Romans 12, and you'll see their goals. Satan wants to make you conform to the world. He wants you amoebic and shapeless, so that you're not really a person, but merely

a result of the environmental influences on you—
the people you know, your glands, all the pressures
of your surroundings. God, on the other hand,
doesn't want you blown by whatever wind comes up
—he wants you conformed to the image of Jesus.
He wants to shape you from within. That's why we
invite Christ **into** our lives. We use that terminology
to stress that Christ works on the **inside** before the
outside. 1 John 4:4 says, "Greater is he who is **in**
you than he that is in the world." While Satan is
exerting pressure from the outside, through your
environment, God is exerting equal pressure inside
to help you keep shape and form.

"You remember the **Thresher,** Neal?" I asked.
"The submarine that was lost in the Atlantic?"

"Sure," Neal said.

"You know what they found? Some of the bulk-
heads hadn't been properly welded, and when the
ship got down to a certain depth they gave way. The
men inside were cooked as if in a pressure cooker.
They say sea water came in as live steam. They
found only small pieces of the **Thresher,** because
the outside pressure was so great that, without a
corresponding pressure from the inside, it was
crumpled like a piece of paper."

That really got to Neal. "That's me," he said,
shaking his head slowly. "But how can I keep the
outside pressures from crumpling me?"

"You'll have to understand the difference between being transformed and conformed," I said.
"Here in camp you're conforming to a Christian

environment; at home you conform to a non-Christian environment. The real issue in Christianity isn't being conformed, but being transformed. Christ didn't come into the world to take you out of the pressure situation. He came to get inside your life and give you inner strength to face it. It'd be worthless to spend all your time at this camp, singing the songs, praying, and fellowshiping with neat Christians. God doesn't want that. That's just another kind of conformity—conformity to a Christian environment. Jesus wants to change you inside, to make you a Christian in more than appearance.''

Neal thought about that for a while. "Jay," he said, "I don't think I'm really a Christian." He'd been to camp; he knew all about the Bible; he could act just like a Christian—but he'd never asked Christ to come inside. That night he did. The next day he left camp, knowing he didn't have to be a chameleon any more.

At this point people ask, "Okay, but what about me? I've asked Christ into my life, but I still feel pressures outside. How come?''

To start with, there is a great deal of difference between those pressures, which we call temptation, and sin. Some Christians wish they were never tempted. They can't take the pressure, and they say, "I want to be taken out of this." Then they become a hothouse plant. They continually search for little groups that are all Christian—they all sing the latest Christian songs, read the latest Christian

books, and have great fellowship—but they're totally useless, because in trying to escape all temptation they've given up their chance to help others.

That's not God's plan. We're all tempted. In fact,
James 1:12 says, "Blessed is the man who endures
temptations, for he shall win the crown of life."
Apparently if you're not tempted, you don't stand a
chance to win the crown of life.

Now what happens when you're tempted? Does
Satan come under the door like a mysterious green
fog? No. He tries to get you in very ordinary ways—
through your body, your mind, your personality,
through relationships. He is trying all the time, and
there's no way to escape it. God doesn't want you to
escape it—he wants you to learn how to handle it.

Take the guy who knows he's a Christian, and
that he's given himself to the Lord. He goes with
his buddies down to the pool and Suzie walks by.
Wham! He learns something new about himself.
He learns that Christian eyes, dissected by a bi-
ologist, are exactly like anyone else's eyes. He
thought that once he became a Christian he wouldn't
see girls the same way. He thought he'd never notice
they have pretty bodies. And now he wants to say,
"What's wrong? I thought I was a Christian."

But nothing's wrong. Not yet. At this point he has
a chance to react as a Christian should, and grow
as a Christian. It's an opportunity and a danger.
There are two voices he can listen to—the voice of
temptation or the voice of the Spirit of Christ, who
is inside him if he's a Christian. If he responds ir-

responsibly and resists the Spirit of Christ, he takes
the image of Suzie and puts it in some moist, warm,
corner of his life where he fondles it, pets it, and
keeps it for future reference.

But there is an alternative. He can say, "Thank
you, Lord, for creating Suzie. She's beautiful, and I
appreciate that, but I want to look on her as a person, not an object. I want to do what Paul told
Timothy to do—to 'see the young women as sisters.'
I want to know her as a total person, with feelings,
pain, aspirations."

If a guy reacts that way, he's grown as a Christian. He's made a step he might never have made
unless he had seen Suzie. He's given a new part of
himself to God. It works a lot better than repressing
the whole thing. Saying "I will not think about girls"
is about as effective as saying "I will not think about
a ten-foot tall pink elephant." If you say you won't
think about it, that's all you'll think of. But if you
acknowledge it, and give it to Christ, you can grow in
grace through overcoming a temptation.

At a **Campus Life** camp in Colorado once, I told
about my behind-the-woodpile conversation with
Neal. Later sixteen fellows got together and shared
about their own lives, and they came to me with a
burning question. "All that stuff about Neal is fine
for guys who are virgins, clean, spotless guys," they
said, "but none of us are in that position. All of us
have already disobeyed God. We've had sex with
girls. We've failed—does that mean we're through,

disqualified from being Christians? Are we ready for the junk pile?''

Of course I told them no. "That's what 1 John 1:9 is all about," I said. "It says if we confess our sins, God will cleanse us from all unrighteousness.''

Peter, Jesus' disciple, had the same confusion those guys had. He couldn't get it through his head that God was so forgiving—that every time you blew it, God was glad to forgive you. He asked Jesus, "How many times do you have to forgive a man, seven times?'' Jesus said no, seventy times seven, or as many times as he comes to you. Now if God expected Peter to forgive that readily, doesn't it follow that God would at least be as forgiving as he expected Peter to be?

Some people have gotten very good at asking for forgiveness, of course. You wonder how sincere they are, because they haven't changed the situations that made them sin in the first place. Fellows, for instance, complain about trouble with their thought life. Sometimes I have to tell them, "Don't come and talk to me about your thought life. You go home and get rid of the girlie books—the ones you have underneath your dresser drawer or up in the attic. Until you've done that, it's pretty hard to believe you want to clean up your thought life.''

Prayer is a great weapon in fighting temptation. When you know a situation is going to be tough, prepare for it by asking God for help. If you're going to be with a bunch of kids who you know like to gossip, for instance, pray that you'll be able to have a good time with them and not gossip. Ask God to help you steer the conversation toward better things.

Scripture helps tremendously. If you know the Bible, if you read it, and think about it, there's good material going into you. The old computer slogan, "Garbage in, garbage out," really applies here. If there's garbage going into your mind, garbage is going to come out, too. Reading and thinking about the Bible gives you a chance to put good stuff into your mind. It helps to read a verse before you go to bed. That gives your mind something to work on while you're asleep.

Temptation demands a positive antidote. You can't waltz into a compromising situation, and then think, "I hope I don't do anything wrong." You need a positive antidote long before then. Get a hobby, get involved, fill up your mind with good things.

And when it comes to resisting temptation, it's amazing how little credit common sense gets. There are practical things you can do in specific situations. If you're tempted to go too far with a girl or guy, for instance, there are specific things you need to watch out for. You start getting into trouble when you plan on spending five hours together, but don't plan what you're going to do. Common sense will tell you what you'll end up doing. If you don't plan your date, and then go too far, don't yell, "The devil made me do it." You asked for trouble.

God wants you to use your head. He wants you to use prayer, to turn to him and his Word when the going gets rough. He wants you to fill your mind and your life with positive, good things. He doesn't want you crushed by the pressures outside your body, but maintained by the Spirit of Christ living inside you. Everyone is tempted, but as 1 Corinthians 10:13 says, no temptation is too great for you to resist. This is God's goal in these pressure situations: by resisting temptation, you'll let him transform you in each area of your life. He wants you to grow as a Christian.

"I can't get ahold of God," he said.
"It's like someone's taken an ice cream stick and
scraped out his insides." (See chapter 1.)

Sometimes I wish I could solve
all my problems by magic.
But Jesus didn't. (See chapter 2.)

Some people say,
"The more weird you are,
the better Christian you must be." (See chapter 3.)

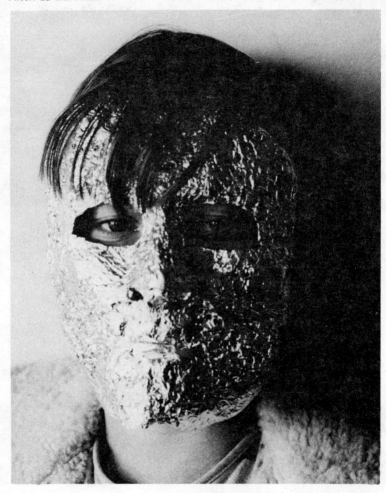

If God opened shop for body alterations,
would you be standing in line? (See chapter 4.)

It's fun to be a
chameleon,
changing colors to
fit your background.
But aren't you
a victim
of your environment?
(See chapter 5.)

Photo: Ed Trenner

I said to mys
if that's the kind of girl they think I
then that's the kind of girl I'm going to be. (See chapter

**Double-mindedness—when you don't know where you're headed.
(See chapter 7.)**

In one small corner of the universe
is a tiny planet where two-legged creatures say,
"I do what I want to do!" (See chapter 8.)

you're holding hands.
at are you going to do for the next six years. (See chapter 9.)

Photo: Rick Kotter

Do you drag somebody to Christ like you'd pull a stubborn animal? (See chapter 10.)

6

how do I
experience forgiveness?

I was walking toward the pool, my towel over my shoulder, and met Linda. "Hello," I said, and she fell on the ground and started crying.

I had no idea what was going on. I sat down next to her and asked what was wrong, but she didn't answer. So I sucked on a blade of grass for a while, and eventually she turned to me. "What's wrong?" I asked.

"I'm the worst girl in the world," she said.

"What on earth makes you think that?" I asked, but she began to cry again. Feeling very awkward, I searched for something to tell her. "You know, there's a lot of competition out there. I could believe you're pretty bad, but the worst girl in the world . . . you'd really have to work at that."

"Don't make fun of me," she said. Then she told me about the past year.

"I was the first sophomore in our school ever to be a cheerleader. I got to go to all the upperclass events and eventually found myself dating a senior, the best basketball player in the school. We went everywhere together. Soon we were going steady.

"Then they had a senior ditch day, and I heard afterwards that my boyfriend had gone with another girl. We had a scene, right in the hall with everyone watching. I threw his ring at him and ran into the washroom and cried. I stayed home from school for two days because I couldn't go and face my friends.

"One evening some girls drove by the house and blew the horn. They weren't the kind of girls I usually hang around with, but I was really low— feeling sorry for myself, and tired of sitting around the house. So I went with them. We drove to a town about twenty miles away and pulled into a drive-in next to some guys. We talked to them and eventually paired off.

"The next day at school there were stories about me all over the place. Kids at my school can be like cannibals. People want to tear you apart, and if you give them any opportunity, they will. The girls told people I'd done things I never had, and everyone believed them. No one would believe me. I said to myself, if that's the kind of girl they think I am, then that's the kind of girl I'm going to be. And for the rest of the year, I've been just that. I'm a mess. I'm the worst girl in the world."

the harper valley pta mentality

As I started talking to Linda, I realized what an

omnipresent problem guilt is. Everybody feels it at times—maybe not as strongly as Linda did but in a real way. We've all done things we're deeply ashamed of.

As I've talked to people again and again in Linda's position, I've seen some good and bad ways of handling guilt.

Some people rationalize it. They blame what they did on other people or circumstances, and pretty soon they rub out the guilt feelings their conscience gave them.

Others say, "Let your conscience be your guide," but I doubt that's wise. Your conscience is a very tameable animal. Adolph Eichmann, who helped destroy six million Jews, showed almost no remorse. He said he would jump into his grave with glee, because he believed he hadn't done anything wrong. He'd tamed his conscience.

One favorite way of taming your conscience is what I call the "Harper Valley PTA" mentality. "Harper Valley PTA" was a song quite a few years ago where a lady who's being put down by PTA members goes to their meeting and tells them how bad **they** are. The implication is, "I'm better than you, because we're all bad, but I don't pretend to be better than what I am. At least I'm honest." Well, being honest doesn't count for much if you're just honest about being bad. You're still bad.

But most people don't handle guilt that way. They may excuse themselves, but when you get beneath the surface, they're like Linda. They're really sorry for what they've done.

That's a necessary starting point. I'd rather see someone broken down with grief than arrogantly refusing to admit wrongdoing, like Eichmann.

But just being sorry doesn't necessarily help. It wasn't helping Linda; in fact, it was destroying her.

how sorry can you get?

Skid row bums are sorry. It used to be quite a sport in Chicago to take visitors down to see them. You would roll up the windows, lock the doors, and drive around looking at the bums lying in the doorways and gutters. You told your children, "Don't point at the men," so you drove along looking at them out of the corners of your eyes. You didn't want to embarrass them.

But if you did what the bums wanted, you'd tell your children, "Point at them! Shame them!" Most of them were on skid row to punish themselves. They were sorry for something they'd done, and were ruining their lives to prove how sorry they were. By shaming them you helped them punish themselves.

But skid row sorrow doesn't help. In fact, it destroys. Second Corinthians 7:8–11 tells us that. Paul's first letter really let the church at Corinth have it, and later he wrote something like, "I'm glad I made you sorry, because it made you repent. Your sorrow was godly sorrow. But there is another kind of sorrow—worldly sorrow. And worldly sorrow leads to death."

The bums on skid row have worldly sorrow. It

is remorse—taking upon yourself the responsibility for something you've done wrong and living with it. Nothing will destroy men faster.

You want to see clear examples of worldly and godly sorrow? Look in the Bible. Two of Jesus' disciples are perfect examples: Judas and Peter.

the world's most unpopular man

Judas is unquestionably the world's most unpopular man. What father ever looked at his newborn son and said, "I think I'll name him Judas"? No man in history is so despised.

But this sometimes makes us paint Judas in the wrong way. We think of him as a sneaky, traitorous, dirty little so-and-so who never had any intention of following Jesus in the first place. That's far from what Judas was like. For one thing, he was the treasurer.

You don't take the sneakiest person in the group and make him treasurer. You couldn't tell the disciples from other people on the street by the halos around their heads. You could tell them, however, by the absence of a bulge where a guy normally carries his billfold. Why? Because all the disciples gave their billfolds to Judas. He was chosen to handle the money for the whole group. They trusted him!

And Judas did choose to follow Jesus. I think he was originally sincere in wanting to help Jesus set up a new kingdom. But once a woman was dumping some perfume on Jesus. It wasn't an Evening in

Paris, $2.98 concoction. It was expensive—some say the equivalent of $5,000 to $10,000 in our day. Well, Judas was incensed. He suggested the money be given to the poor. (Though John says he wanted the money himself.) Jesus rebuked him. He told him they'd have plenty of time to help the poor, but not much time to glorify him before he was gone. It put Judas off, and his faith in Jesus went down from that point.

But lots of people missed Jesus' point. Peter did, too, even though he was in the disciples' inner three. He was one of the very few men in history to hear the audible voice of God, when God said, "This is my beloved Son, hear him." But that didn't keep him from making mistakes. He missed the point of Jesus' life so badly once that Jesus said to him, "Get behind me, Satan."

At the time of Jesus' crucifixion, tremendous pressure was put on both these men. Judas had been steadily losing faith in Jesus, and he did the worst thing possible—he betrayed Jesus for thirty pieces of silver. He felt guilty, and after they arrested Jesus he tried to undo it by giving the money back. But the Pharisees wouldn't take it. They laughed at him and made fun. With their laughter ringing in his ears, he threw the money down and ran out of the room. He felt absolutely awful. He thought of James and John and the big fisherman Peter. He'd spent three years with them, and now, how could he ever face them again?

the big fisherman blew it

About the same time Judas was thinking that, Peter was going through a similar crisis. He had just told Jesus that he would never desert him, and when Jesus was arrested, he had followed behind him even though everyone else had run. Maybe he hoped to rescue him. He waited outside while Jesus was on trial, warming his hands at a fire.

A girl asked him if he were one of Jesus' followers. Peter got scared, and he swore that he wasn't. It happened twice more that night—he did what he knew was wrong, what he'd sworn never to do—he denied knowing anything about Jesus at all. Suddenly he heard the rooster crow, and he remembered Jesus had predicted he'd deny him, just that way. Peter fell apart. Peter, the big, strong fisherman, ran out weeping bitterly.

Judas and Peter had both blown it—and they both were sorry. But how did they respond to their guilt? Judas was determined to demonstrate how sorry he was. Eventually he thought of a plan that would prove it. No one would ever be able to deny he was sorry for betraying Jesus. He went as far as any man can go to prove his regret; he went out and killed himself. Scripture leaves no doubt that Judas is separated from God today. He was sorry, but his sorrow wasn't godly sorrow.

Peter's was. Was he more sincere than Judas? I doubt it. But the next time we see him, he's preaching at Pentecost, bringing thousands of people to faith in Jesus. What's the difference?

The difference is in the object of the sorrow. The remorseful man puts all the blame on himself, and keeps it there. He wants it to weigh him down so he and everyone else will know he's sorry. That's what Judas did.

But the repentant man—the man who's sorry in God's way—puts the guilt and the pain on the cross by trusting Jesus' forgiveness. He leaves it there, and goes on following Jesus. That's what Peter did.

People in southern Indiana tell a story about a man riding down the road on a donkey, carrying a 200-pound sack of wheat on his shoulders. A man asked him, "Why don't you take the weight off your own shoulders and put it on the donkey?" He said back, "You don't think I'm going to ask the donkey to carry all that weight, do you?"

I think a lot of people are the same way. They hear Jesus say, "Come to me all you who are heavily burdened, and I'll give you rest" (Matt. 11:28), and they decide to go to him. But they still carry the burden of all the things they're sorry for. They're like people washing up to take a bath. You don't clean up before you take a bath; you take the bath for the purpose of getting clean. It's the same with guilt. You don't clean up your own guilty life through self-sacrifice, self-punishment, and self-destruction so that God can accept you. You go to God first and let him clean things up. Sorrow and self-pity really don't please God at all. In fact, they get in his way.

What he wants is godly sorrow that repentantly brings things to him and lets him keep them.

from a bug to a butterfly

That's the story I told Linda. I told her about Peter and Judas, and when I got done I said, "Would you like to pray?" She did. She said, "God, I'm embarrassed about all these things. I've tried very hard to tell you I'm sorry. I've been doing these things because I felt so bad about myself . . . I've been trying to hurt myself. I know that Jesus died on the cross for my sins. He was destroyed for my sins, and I can't get rid of my sins by destroying myself. So help me, God, to accept that and follow you."

It transformed her. Maybe you've read the story Franz Kafka wrote, **The Metamorphosis.** It tells about a man who woke up one morning, having turned into a bug. This was just the opposite. Linda thought she was a bug, and she turned into a butterfly right before my eyes. Suddenly she looked beautiful, and her whole outlook was different. She'd stopped holding onto that sorrow, and let it go. She was ready to follow Jesus.

Your whole life as a Christian will be full of moments like that. God knows you are going to blow it. He was aware of that the moment you first came into his family, but it didn't make him kick you out.

Repentance is a constant relationship with God. You don't have to hide sin in a moldy corner. You don't have to work up to a big, emotional "I'm sorry" scene. You just have to learn to walk in a spirit of repentance, where you're more and more aware of how far short you are of what God wants, but also aware that God will forgive you and give you the power to overcome. That's what godly sorrow is about. Instead of leading to death, as remorse does, it leads to life—forgiven, free, precious life.

7

make up your mind

We were at a church youth meeting.

"When I'm here," she said, "I'm thinking about what the other kids are out doing. I know they're having a ball and I'm totally out of it. When we get to school on Monday they'll be talking about what they did, and I'll be thinking about how I spent my time in a church.

"But when I do go out with them and do what they do, I feel guilty. I think about my pastor, my parents, and my Christian friends, and I know they wouldn't look up to me. So I feel miserable there, too. It just seems hopeless. I'm miserable wherever I go."

Her problem may be the most common malady among Christians. It's called "double-mindedness." Have you felt it? As though one foot is on the pier and the other in the canoe? It's like playing football when one opponent has one of your legs and another has the other leg, and you hear one of them say, "Make a wish." You want to act like a Christian, but you feel

like acting like a non-Christian, too. You don't want
to completely commit yourself just yet.

It's not a new problem. You can read about people facing it all through the Bible. One couple, Ananias and Sapphira, died because they couldn't
handle it.

At that time Roman taxes were causing an eco-
nomic depression. The Christians got hit harder
than anybody else, so they were sharing everything
they had. Sometimes in a government class you'll
hear this referred to as the first time communism
appeared on the earth. Well, these people didn't
know communism from rheumatism. They simply
didn't think it was a good thing to see other people
starve. So they sold their property and used the
money to help each other.

This couple, Ananias and Sapphira, decided to
sell some land and bring the money to the church to
be divided up. That was what a lot of people were
doing. But after they sold the land they began to
wonder whether it was really a good idea. What if
some kind of emergency hit them? So they decided
to go halfway. They kept some of the money themselves and brought the rest to church, pretending
it was the full amount.

Ananias arrived at church about three hours
ahead of his wife. He presented the money to Peter.
But Peter knew it wasn't the full amount. "Why are
you doing this?" he said. "You didn't have to. Wasn't
it strictly voluntary to sell the land in the first place?
You aren't lying to me, you know. You're lying to

God himself!'' And at those words Ananias fell down dead, and they took him out and buried him.

Three hours later Sapphira came in. Peter asked her, "Is this how much you got for the land?'' She said, "Yes.'' Peter said, "Here come the men who just buried your husband for telling the same lie. They'll carry you out, too.'' And Sapphira fell down and died. The Bible says that "great fear'' came upon the church.

It's not hard to imagine why. Evidently God doesn't choose to work that way today, but can you imagine if he did? Can you hear someone saying, "Man, down at First Methodist, they don't mess around. You tell a fib, and it's all over.''

Of course, there's a lot of the story we don't know. We don't know if Ananias and Sapphira were really Christians. We don't know if there were other things they had done. But you can see one thing: they wanted to trust in God, but not trust in him 100 percent. It couldn't be done. They had to choose.

living through a keyhole

Some Christians will try to tell you the world's way of living isn't pleasurable. That's nonsense. If sin weren't pleasurable, there'd be no conflict. It isn't sinning that makes you miserable—it's trying to live with your conscience when you're sinning. If you could be totally committed to sin as a way of life, you wouldn't have this problem. Of course, that's the short-term view. In the long run your life would be literally hell. But for right now, sin is fun. It's the Christians who get involved in sin who are miserable. They've closed the door on sin and then spend their lives looking through the keyhole.

A Christian in this position reminds me of how people in some parts of the world catch monkeys. They drill a hole in a coconut and scrape out all the inside. Then they put in a small piece of candy. When the monkey comes along he sticks his hand into the hole, which is just big enough for his arm, and he grabs the sweet. Then he discovers he has a problem. He can't get his fist out of the hole. The only way he can get out is to let go of the candy.

But he's too greedy for that. He'll scream and bang the coconut around, but he won't let go. Eventually a hunter will come along, bang him on the head and put him in a sack. It's safe to assume that the monkey wanted to stay away from the hunter a lot more than he wanted the candy. But he wouldn't make the choice. It ended up ruining him.

In humans we call this double-mindedness. James says a double-minded man is unstable in everything he does. He can't or won't make up his mind, so he's gradually corrupted in everything. Everything! Sometimes people think that it'll just corrupt part of them, maybe their religious life. But it isn't so.

1. Double-mindedness corrupts your relationship with yourself. You can fool other people most of the time, but you can't fool yourself. If you look in the mirror and find yourself as phony as a $3.00 bill,

you lose self-respect. You begin to feel that other people are watching you, even if they're not. You punish yourself.

2. Double-mindedness corrupts your relationship with other people. People see through you more than you think. If you say you're a Christian and then don't act that way, others are going to notice it. They won't take you seriously when you say something.

I saw an example of this at camp once. There was a girl who was constantly asking that we pray for her friends, her boyfriend, for all kinds of people. She was almost uncomfortably religious. Every time we'd ask for some feedback after a talk she'd be the first one to respond.

One night during a meeting her boyfriend and some other guys showed up at the camp. They were rough-looking guys, riding motorcycles, and they came into the meeting and sat in the back. At the end we asked those who wanted to commit themselves to Christ to come into a room off the side to talk, and this girl came forward. I wondered at the time, "Why her?" since she seemed like such a super saint. But I got to talk to her along with her boyfriend, who had followed her up to the front.

"I've been a real phony," she said. She told me she and her boyfriend had been involved in this and that together, and how ashamed they were. She was crying, and she looked at him and cried some more and then talked to me some more. Then she said she really wanted to be 100 percent—to give her life entirely to Christ and not be phony any more.

Her boyfriend interrupted and said, "Do you really mean that?" He couldn't believe it.

But she said she really did. "I mean it so much that if you don't want to have anything to do with me any more, that's okay. I still want to be a Christian."

So he said to me, "Do me, too!" He wanted to give himself to Christ. "I never thought you meant it about being a Christian," he told her. "I thought it was just something you did for your folks, and when we got together it was different. But if it means that much to you there must be something to it. I want to get a look at it myself." So I spent the next hour or so explaining it to him, and he prayed to accept Christ. Up until then he'd seen only double-mindedness. When he saw genuine, total commitment, he knew there was something very different about it.

3. Double-mindedness corrupts your relationship to God. God is more concerned with a sincere, committed heart than anything else. How we act is important, but it isn't worth a thing if it's just for show. The Bible says that David was a man after God's own heart. But David did everything wrong you can think of. He was an adulterer and a murderer. But he was really committed to God, and God loved him for that despite some tragic mistakes.

You're not fooling God if your commitment to him

isn't total. Sometimes we use our relationship to God as a sort of fire escape for emergencies. We don't want God to disconnect the phone, but we'd rather he didn't call us up all the time, either. The joy of relating to him goes away. Soon there's only a shell we're putting up for other people.

eternal toothache

You have to decide between two kinds of pain. One is the pain of total surrender—of saying, "Christ, I really want to do what you want, and nothing is going to stand in my way any longer. You're the most important thing in my life." That is painful sometimes. You may have to give up some things you don't want to give up. But it's like the pain of having a tooth pulled—you dread it and worry about it, but you know sooner or later you have to face up to it.

Because if you don't face that pain, you get the pain of double-mindedness. It's like a toothache that never stops. It may not be as excruciating, but it's a gnawing, agonizing pain. The person who is a Christian but is living with this pain can spend his whole life with a sense of worthlessness, because he won't make the total commitment to Christ that's necessary.

That commitment is different for everybody. There are certain areas, however, which are key ones for students. One is the kind of friends you are going to spend your time with. Some aren't affected by people around them—in fact, they thrive in an adverse environment. They tend to affect the people around them much more than they're affected. But others absorb whatever environment they're in. If you're one of those in the latter category, your complete commitment to Christ may involve cutting off old friendships and finding a new social circle. It will be painful, don't kid yourself that it won't. But if you're going to lose the pain of double-mindedness, it may have to be done.

Another crucial area for some kids is in the habits they've picked up. I'm thinking particularly of drugs and alcohol. Don't pretend to yourself that you're committed to Christ when you're abusing your body. Do you trust Christ to provide what you need, or don't you? If you do, then you don't need crutches.

And are you going to trust God to give you the ideal sex life inside marriage, with the ideal partner of his choice? Or are you going to mess around with the opposite sex trying to provide for yourself? God wants us to be pure sexually, and as a Christian you know it. But are you sufficiently committed to him to act like it?

Maybe you've started thinking about your goals in life. If God wants something from you that will contribute to other people more than just making money, are you ready for it? Are you willing to make it your goal, to work and plan for it? Or will you goof off, take the easy courses and get by? Are you going to do the best you can? It isn't easy to work hard at school. But if God wants you to be doing something worthwhile for him in life, it's probably going to be necessary.

There are a lot of other issues. Maybe it's a commitment to pray and study the Bible regularly that you need to make. Wishing it's so isn't enough. Any choice you make for commitment to Christ is going to cost something.

Now, if you give yourself totally to Christ, that doesn't mean that it's done for all time. Total commitment has been defined as giving all you know of yourself to all you know of God. It's only natural that as you learn more about yourself and God, new commitments will have to be made. It'll be necessary again and again.

Giving yourself totally to Christ doesn't guarantee that you'll never sin again, either. You won't always do what you want to do. But at least if you've decided for Christ it will be clean-cut. When you blow it, you'll know you blew it. There'll be no doubt. You can ask forgiveness from God and get back on the right track. Your mind will still be set in the right direction. You won't be caught in the middle of two desires.

I'm convinced this is the key to real mental health. A person who really knows what he wants in life, who is going toward that and isn't trying to do two things at once, is going to be pretty stable. Not that he's a fanatic. He can be aware of his own failings, and he can have a sense of humor about what he's doing.

But he's made the choice. He's chosen to live for

Christ because that's the only thing in life that's worthwhile. He's seen that it means giving up some other very pleasurable things that aren't good for him. And he's given them up. He's given himself up, totally, to Jesus Christ.

8

why do
terrible things happen?

Jimmy was a big guy who played tackle for Red-mont High School. One night over coffee he told me about his girlfriend. "We've been going together for almost a year, and the whole time I've been praying that she become a Christian. But she hasn't. How come?"

Kay, a small, mousy girl with a cute smile, wasn't smiling when she came to talk to me. "I can't believe in God any more," she said, and she started to cry. Her little sister had drowned in a flood. She'd seen the swollen body when they finally found it down-river. She asked me, "Why would God let that happen? If he's in control of everything, and he loves everybody, why should he let Patty get killed?"

Ray's problem wasn't as serious, and he tried to joke about it in the group. But you could tell it was bothering him. Pimples. Why, oh why, did God let people have pimples? It would be so easy just to wipe them out.

Susan came up to me one night after I spoke. "I can't believe in the God you talk about," she said. "He's trivial. All he cares about is whether people drink and smoke dope. He doesn't care about thirty million people starving to death. He didn't do anything about Hitler."

why doesn't he do something?

Sooner or later, most people end up asking this kind of question. If God loves everybody, why doesn't he stop bad things from happening?

Usually it hits you very suddenly. You read **The Diary of Anne Frank**, or your dad dies, or you see a film on starving children, and you're faced with the question: Why isn't God more involved?

To understand this, I start with three stories Jesus told in Luke 15: the stories of the lost sheep, the lost coin, and the lost youth (better known as the Prodigal Son).

In the sheep story, one sheep is lost. The shepherd leaves all the rest of the sheep behind and searches for it. He finds it, brings it home, and everybody's ecstatic. The same with the lost coin: the woman searches the house until she finds it and puts it in a safe place. But the lost youth is different: when he's lost, the father stays home and waits for him to return.

Now, how come when a sheep's lost, the shepherd goes after it; when a coin's lost, the lady looks for it; but when a kid's lost, the father stays home? Isn't the boy as valuable as a sheep or a coin? Obviously he is.

Then why doesn't Jesus have the father go after him?

He doesn't go after him because he's applying a principle people know better from their day-to-day living than from their theology: force doesn't work with human beings. If the father got a big, mean servant to go and drag the kid home, then threw him in the back bedroom and said, "You can come out when you're ready to fly right," the kid would sit on the edge of the bed and say, "You just wait until I get out of this bedroom. I'm going right back where I was. I was ready to make a big success of myself. It's just like my dad to interfere, right when I was going to make it."

The lesson would never be learned. So the father has to wait at home, worried sick, until the kid wakes up. He has to come to that point by himself.

That's the difference between objects and men. Man has a choice whether to live in harmony with God or not. Sheep and coins do not. If God wants to have man love him, he won't use coercion. He could light up the sky with letters forty miles high and convincingly prove he existed. But the very experience of seeing that would make you more like a sheep or a coin than a man. It would wipe you out; you'd have no choice but to respond to him.

Imagine a guy who wants to get a girl to love him.

Probably the guy is strong enough to overpower the girl. He could, just by brute strength, get the girl to do anything he wanted her to do. But he doesn't. He wants a love relationship. He doesn't want a robot who will do what he wants if he twists her arm enough. He wants her to respond willingly. That can never happen if he takes away her power to resist him. He has to offer himself gently and without force.

Now what does this have to do with a girl whose little sister drowned? Just this: God could stop that. He could overpower the world, killing all the Stalins and Hitlers, lifting little girls up out of the flood-water, curing everybody in all the hospitals. He could do that, but he doesn't. If he did, we'd be so shattered we'd **have** to fall to our knees and worship him. We'd have no choice as to whether to love him or not. It wouldn't be a love relationship; it would be rape. It would ruin the human project.

You see, God has a number of projects. He has the plant project, the fish project, the animal project, and the man project. Each project is meant to glorify God. The human project is different from the others in that God made man to respond voluntarily to what God wants. And man has rejected that. The Bible traces it back to the beginning of time, when the first man and woman rejected God, chose their own way, and made a mess of themselves and their planet.

the universe is in harmony

Now think a little while about what an incredible

thing this is. The whole universe is in harmony with God. It glorifies God by doing what it's designed to do in an orderly fashion. The stars don't just zoom around up there. People predict things by them. They steer ships by them. By them they tell the exact time, more accurately than any ordinary clock could.

And it's a huge universe. If you could make a spaceship that would go the speed of light, it would take you only eight minutes to get to the sun from our planet. But you could spend 50,000 years traveling in our galaxy. To get to the next galaxy would take about a million years. Then if you got bored and wanted to go to the next galaxy, you'd have to go some 2–6 billion years.

This unthinkably huge universe moves in perfect order. It's in perfect harmony with what God wants. But over in one corner, one little speck called Earth, one of the smallest of the planets, has these two-legged things that have the right to stand up on their hind legs in the middle of all that order and say, "I do what I want to do because I want to do it, and God had better leave me alone." And God listens to them if they say that, and he will leave them alone.

Take a look at a tree. It's a beautiful thing, tremendously complex. It's part of the rain cycle, part of the oxygen/carbon-dioxide cycle. All the tremendously complex and perfect aspects of a tree glorify God, but do it involuntarily. A tree can't stand there and say, "I will not participate in the carbon-dioxide cycle." It has to. Man, however, can say that. He can commit suicide; he can completely disrupt the peaceful world God has in mind for him.

Now why did God give that right? Why, out of all the creatures in the universe, did he give that right to disrupt things to man? It must be that voluntary cooperation, the love that man can give God, is incredibly valuable. God lets our planet be a potential sore in the universe so that humans can choose to be everything they're meant to be by choosing him. It's a tremendously valuable thing to God.

it's not what I've heard

When most people hear this, they're excited by it, but they say, "Jay, that's great, but it doesn't sound like the God I've always heard about." And that's true a lot of the time. If we're not careful, we end up with a God who is nothing more than the sum of our experiences. This is what primitive man does: every time he has an experience, he goes out and carves a face on his totem pole. A tornado wipes out his house, and he carves a big scowling face. A flood comes, same thing. Pretty soon he has a totem pole composed of scowling faces, and his image of God is a very hostile, frightening one.

Things are different in our time. Science and technology make most of us safe from catastrophes. They put a roof over our head and food in our stomach. So the faces we carve on our totem pole are smiling. We find a parking space, God is smiling. We get a good grade, God is smiling. But this image of

God isn't any more valuable than the scowling one, because it's based only on our experiences. If our closest friend dies, or we flunk a few classes, the faces on the totem pole may change their expressions. We need to get beyond our day-to-day experiences with nature and environment and discover the real God who made all these objects.

God, you see, doesn't pick up one car on the freeway and smash it into another. He doesn't ordinarily disintegrate a car occupying your favorite parking space, either. We say he isn't normally casually related to such things. He doesn't ordinarily reshuffle the universe just to please us. If we're traveling at excessive speeds, and we've had a few to drink, he doesn't often magically hold the car on course.

When people hear this, they get nervous. They think God's control of the universe is being threatened. They think I'm limiting God. But I'm not. God could easily lift that car and place it back on course just as it goes over the embankment. But because he will not force men to look at him, because he wants to leave us a choice whether to obey him or not, he doesn't. He still rules the universe, but he rules it through physical laws such as the law of gravity. These laws he seldom interferes with.

he weeps, too

You think it's rotten that your little sister drowned in a flood, her head banged against pilings and trees, her lungs suffocating in water? God does, too! He weeps! Jesus wept at the death of Lazarus, his friend. He sweat blood thinking about his own death. He didn't think it was neat. He thought death was awful.

But he also thought there were worse things. One worse thing would be for his Father to forfeit the chance to have men willingly, voluntarily love him. He could have asked his Father to make a physical assault on the earth, wiping out death then and there, forcing men to acknowledge him. But he considered our humanness more precious than anything else.

With this in mind, I can help a girl like Kay, whose sister drowned, to understand that God still loves her, and even loves her little sister. He's not punishing her for something by killing her sister, and he's not a savage, hostile God. Kay doesn't have to believe it's great that her sister died, either. Understanding who God is and how he's involved with her should let her see God's unimaginably glorious scheme: the voluntary love relationships between man and his God, the cooperation with God that's more than a plant's—the willing giving of yourself to God because of who he is.

Of course, this barely scratches the surface of the questions about God's involvement with man. You may have said, "Hey wait a minute" several times as you read. If so, I'd particularly recommend **Mere Christianity** and **The Problem of Pain,** both by C. S. Lewis. These are pretty heavy reading—but they dig into the questions in a much deeper fashion than it's possible to do here.

It's for sure there aren't any simple answers. But by asking the questions and digging deep, we learn a lot about God and the way he wants to relate to us. It gets us away from a flippant, easy-answer approach to Jesus, and draws us closer to the real God who made this universe—and us.

What a fantastic thing this is! We have the chance for a love relationship—an intimate, giving friendship—with the God who made the vastness of the galaxies. He respects us as men and women. He will not violate our right to refuse him, yet stands ready to welcome us into his family.

9

sex

Someone once said sex problems are life problems. A guy comes to see me and says, "I think I have a problem, I'm over-sexed." So I say, "Okay, let's talk about it." After a while it begins to come out he has tremendous anxieties about life. Those anxieties are forcing him to look desperately for security, for answers to his doubts. Very often he turns in the direction of sex. Then he has a "sex" problem. But is it really a sex problem?

Take, for instance, the guy who thinks he has to be Marvin Makeout, always going from one girl to the next. He conquers one, then on to the next one. What's the problem? Often you find he doubts if he's really masculine, and if he can really succeed in life. Girls become challenges to him—opportunities to prove he's really a man. He "proves" it so often he begins to think something's wrong. He's got the wrong glands, he thinks, or some hormone is working overtime.

Girls have similar problems. Typically, a girl beginning high school finds her body maturing, but not necessarily at the same rate as her friends'. Some mature faster than she. She worries that she's not going to be a real woman. At the same time she's struggling with problems of the magazine image for girls. She sees ads for bust development, and she begins to wonder, "Am I really adequate?"

Besides, she has a deep desire for security and love. She wonders, "Do I really have it? Will men ever find me attractive?" So she experiments to find out. She tries out different kinds of clothes. Usually she does it rather naively; she doesn't understand why guys react the way they do. But she finds that certain kinds of clothes attract boys. She enjoys the attention. Eventually she finds herself going with one boy, spending a lot of time with him, feeling securely attached to him. Inevitably problems come up—they get too involved in sex, or one of them gets bored or jealous. She may feel trapped by a stifling relationship. She may think there's something wrong with her for not being satisfied with just one guy. So she thinks, "I've got a sex problem." But it isn't a sex problem at all. It's a life problem.

a separate world

Why the confusion? Because sex isn't put into a whole–life concept in our world. It's put into a separate box. Sex is depicted as a pleasure machine. It has very little to do with people. It only involves bodies and skin.

The truth is, however, that the free-sex people didn't invent sex. God did. He thought the whole thing up.

God designed sex to be in marriage—a climate in which two human beings come together in the middle of a very hostile world to offer their love to each other. In that healing climate, the two are involved in intimacies and expressions of love so private they share total oneness. They create a small kingdom where the hostilities of the world can't get to them.

And the language of this world is called sex. Through it these two persons communicate and become one. In this context it's truly beautiful. Who wouldn't want it?

area of frustration

Two people going together today face more sexual pressures than ever before in history. I think the best way to show the pressure is to imagine a graph. The horizontal line I call the line of duration. On it you put the ages between fourteen and twenty-two. The other line, the vertical line, I call the line of intensity. I put some labels on this line according to how intense the relationship is: you start with dating, go up to steady dating, going steady, going so steady you can't get out of it, engaged to be engaged, engaged, and end with marriage.

In every school there are certain levels of intimacy associated with those levels. For instance, on a first date you might just hold hands. But you might do quite a bit more than that, too. Every school is different. At most schools the average kids hold hands and kiss on the first date.

Then you get up to steady dating. The average person in America, if he's steadily dating, is certainly holding hands and kissing. Chances are it goes a little beyond that. Let's say the average person does a little necking.

Then you talk about going steady—a somewhat official agreement that you belong to each other unless one of you cancels the agreement. Suppose two kids go steady for six months at your school. They'll probably hold hands, kiss, neck—and they may get into petting.

Necking is defined as caressing above the neck; petting below. It may be they even do more than that. Some certainly will.

So when you consider this vertical line of intensity, you find that the higher you go up it, the more you have intimate relationships. One of the rules of the line of intensity is that you always move up, you never move down. The first time you hold hands it's terrific—you don't even want to wash the hand when you get home. But if you've held the same hand 9,000 times, all you get is sweat. It's the same with kissing. The first time you kiss, it's fantastic. But after a while that gets boring, too. So you keep moving up the line of intensity, looking for more intimate ways to say things.

That's what is behind all this: the desire to say something. Most of us aren't poets who can really express ourselves with words. We need physical ways to say things. To touch someone says something. To kiss says a little more. To neck or pet or make love—that says a lot more.

Suppose you're sixteen years old, and you're going steady. In the average school that means you are probably holding hands, kissing, probably necking, and perhaps petting. So put yourself on this graph—draw a line up from sixteen to the level of intimacy: going steady.

Now suppose you think you're in love, and you want to get married some day. When do you plan on having the wedding? That probably depends on what you want to do for the rest of your life. If you go to college, you won't be out until you're about twenty-two. Then you can get married. So draw a line up from age twenty-two to marriage on the line of intimacy. (See graph on page 106.)

Now, connect the points. You get a four-sided closed curve I call the Area of Frustration. It's the number of years you have to wait multiplied by the level of intimacy you're already at. The more intimate the level you're at now, the more frustration is built in. The frustration can be absolutely intolerable, and it makes people do things they wouldn't otherwise do. Either a couple starts going all the

way, or they find a method for mutual satisfaction—
oral sex, mutual masturbation, or something else—
or they break up. Whatever they do probably involves
building up guilt and unhappiness.

arc of responsibility

Is there another alternative? There is. I call it the
Arc of Responsibility, whereby you plan to gradually increase the intensity of your relationship at a
rate that makes you ready for marriage at the right
time and not before. Basically, that means making
decisions about sex, necking, and petting. It means
realizing that sex will still be there tomorrow. You
limit your intimacy now—and you also limit your
frustration. There will still be some frustration,
that's part of life. But it'll be greatly reduced. You'll
be left with a much better chance to get to know
each other as people. You'll have a much better
chance to get along as a couple and end up without
hate or guilt.

the sex trigger

Part of moving along the Arc of Responsibility involves understanding what the opposite sex is like.
People don't all respond to sex in the same way.
They don't even respond to the same things. For a
guy, the sex trigger tends to be the eye or the mind's
eye—what he sees or imagines. Most guys spend a
lot of time in a fantasy world, and one of the favorite
subjects in a fantasy world is sex. Guys aren't always able to cope in the world in which they live, so

they create a mental world where they are King Kong. Then, often, they have problems with masturbation. The root problem isn't masturbation, however, it's life. It's a life problem, not a sex problem. The degree to which they learn to cope with life is the degree to which masturbation can stop being a problem, because masturbation is an escape. Like drugs, like alcohol, it offers a world that's less complex.

For a girl, the sex trigger is often a caress, a touch, or even in deep feelings about love, security, home, and family. That's one reason guys and girls going together develop problems—they don't understand how their opposite reacts. A girl, not understanding a guy's problems, will often dress provocatively on a date. She doesn't necessarily understand that it's provocative, maybe it's just the style. Plenty of girls are trying the bra-less look. But whether she realizes it or not, it starts the guy's motor running as soon as he sees her.

So right from the start, the guy is building up steam in his tank. His imagination is working overtime. The girl doesn't even realize it: she's thinking about where they're going, how much the food is going to cost, how much she dares order.

Then later, after the date, they go some place and begin to neck. She begins to get a few bubbles rising in her tank, too. He's already got quite a head of steam.

Somebody said boys will give love to get sex; girls will give sex to get love. The guy's imagination has been feeding him thoughts on sex: he'll act loving. The girl wants love: she'll act sexy. They both misunderstand the other, and trouble results.

any alternative?

The alternative is to work at understanding and respecting each other as people. To set goals and standards together. You don't get a runaway truck under control when it's racing down a hill; you need to start long before then. Learn to help each other. Make some realistic plans about what you want to accomplish when you're together. Don't just go "out." Go somewhere to do something specific. If you don't set your plans, your glands will set them for you.

But this may involve changing your attitude. Perhaps you'll have to learn to see the opposite sex as persons and not objects.

I listened to a radio show not long ago where a group of cheerleaders were talking about sex. Their general conclusion was you can't trust any guy. They said guys would always go as far as they could possibly get away with, it was up to the girls to draw the line.

Listening to it, I was a little ashamed to be a male. We've acted so poorly that girls talk about us like we're a bunch of slobbering boars. They have to control us because we're so undisciplined we can't control ourselves.

But control comes as part of seeing the opposite sex as real people. Girls ought to be expecting more from guys than an animal-like sex mania. Guys ought to look for more in a girl than a sex object to inflate their ego. Too many guys treat girls like we used to treat bacteria cultures in biology . . . once we were through with them, we threw them in the trash can.

Christianity is the only convincing answer to this. When Christ comes in, you begin to see yourself as really important, so important that God sent his Son to die on the cross for your sins. As a human being, you're the pinnacle of his creation, like the cherry on the sundae. When you respect yourself and other people that way, you're not likely to view them as objects.

That's why Paul wrote to Timothy, "Treat the young women as sisters." Now most normal, healthy guys think that's dumb. Treat the girls at school like they were sisters? Who wants to have a love relationship with his sister?

But Paul's not talking about love in the romantic sense. He's talking about love in the human sense. That kind of love is always necessary before romantic love is possible. A guy claims to love a girl but doesn't even give her basic respect as a person? He's kidding her, and maybe kidding himself. You have to love your opposite as a brother or sister if you're ever going to love him or her properly as a lover.

indian love song

We need a whole new outlook on love. Western man has worked up this idea that you shop around for sex and sort of peddle your own wares. You're looking for the right vibes. If the vibes aren't there, too bad. There's no commitment. It's like sorting potatoes, looking for the one without a blemish. You keep sorting through them, tossing the blemished ones aside until eventually you've gone through the whole sack of potatoes. This idea goes even beyond the wedding ceremony, so we see people with multiple divorces. Why? Because when you find out your partner has blemishes you didn't think were there, and the vibes aren't all they might be, you're going to fall out of love.

In Jesus' culture, it wasn't a problem. They didn't have teenagers as such. They tell us that Mary, his mother, might have been thirteen when she gave birth to him. I've never read anywhere that she might have been over fifteen. Girls just didn't wait that long to get married.

Nor did people go around looking for the right "vibes" back then. Your parents made the decision about whom you were going to marry. There was no anxiety about whom you were going to be in love with, or whether anyone was ever going to marry you. You were going to get married. You were going to love, because love was commitment.

That idea still holds in India. Now, with Western films coming into India, the Indian people get quite worried. They censor many of them. Are they worried about seeing some nudity? Not as I understand it. You can see that on the streets every day. They're worried that their society will be permeated with the

Western idea of love. They don't want that. They think their own systems of commitment work pretty well. They think our idea of love is a disaster. I'm inclined to think they're right.

So can we drop 400 years off the calendar? Can we go back to a culture where our parents choose our mates? No, of course not. But we can be smart enough to recognize the problem. We can be smart enough to develop our own mature concept of love as commitment. We can stop worrying so much about finding Mr. or Miss Perfect, and start worrying more about the level to which we are able to unselfishly commit ourselves to another person.

why wait?

Of course, in the biblical system of marriage, "waiting" for marriage wasn't much of a problem.

Anybody can "wait" until they're thirteen or fourteen.

But it's an incredible problem today. Waiting is probably one of the most difficult things any culture can expect of you. It requires unbelievable poise, self-esteem, confidence, and faith. Not just waiting for sex—waiting for anything. Waiting for the time when you'll be an adult and run your own life is difficult. Waiting in line at the store is hard.

But why wait? If it's hard, why bear the pain? Lots of kids don't, and despite all the scare stories, they're still going strong.

When I was a kid they used to give three reasons: **detection, infection, conception.** Most kids pay no attention to those reasons now. Detection? Well, nobody has to know. There are lots of ways to hide sex from your parents or whomever else you don't want to know.

Of course, there's a negative to that. Even if you don't get caught, what does it do to you to live a double life? You live one life of respectability with your family and another role with your friends. Lincoln said you can't fool all the people all of the time, but I'm not sure that's true. Some people come pretty close. But I do know this, you can't fool yourself. Not all the time. The double life has to bother you.

Infection—is this just an outdated scare story? Everybody has seen the VD films and knows all about prevention. But still the statistics show a phenomenal rise in VD, not a decrease. We do have penicillin now, though, and if you go to the doctor with VD, he'll cure it. So there is a limited sense in which this problem's been cured.

Conception—same story. The rates of unwanted pregnancies are way up, not down, despite all the pills and prophylactics. Nevertheless, theoretically, you can prevent it. Lots of people don't succeed at preventing it, but it's possible.

There are still some sobering things to consider about **detection, infection,** and **conception,** but basically the problems aren't insurmountable any more. Most kids aren't going to wait for sex just on the basis of those old horror stories. The sexual revolution has told us all again and again that sex before marriage can be a beautiful thing. Responsible sex is sex when you use a contraceptive. Are they right? Is there any compelling reason to wait?

talk to the experts

There are a lot of answers to that, mostly tied to the idea that responsible sex means treating each other totally as human beings, not as objects. But those arguments are subtle. I think that for a biblically based Christian it really comes down to a rather arbitrary choice: do you or do you not believe that God expressed the total truth in Jesus Christ as we find him in the New Testament?

If you don't believe this, you may still be a Christian. There are Christians who aren't biblically based. If so, you're on your own. It's up to you to figure things out. Bear in mind the bumper sticker—"the life you save may be your own." Read a lot of Ann Landers, talk to as many sources as possible. Make sure you get the total story, though, visit a V.A. hospital, and talk to guys with VD. Talk to girls who had sex with half a dozen guys before they got married. Talk to the third person in a love triangle—the one who got left behind. Get some good information, and find out if premarital sex is all it's cracked up to be.

If you are a biblically based Christian, though, you're with me. We believe something others don't. We believe God created us, so he knows all about us. We believe that in the Bible he gave us something called revelation. Revelation like a light flashing on in total darkness.

Wandering around in the dark you get lots of information, you fall over a chair here, and you know a piece of information. You bump into the wall—that's more information. But when the light comes on, it's beyond information.

Revelation is like that, because it's an insight that comes from a Supreme Being who sees everything about the incredibly complex nature of the world, past, present, and future. He sees things we can never find out by ourselves.

There was a time a few years ago when everyone thought every disease could be cured by biochemistry. Now you can't find a doctor who believes that. Medicine is just beginning to see the complex relationship between man's mind and his body. I talked to a doctor who said 80 percent of his patients are suffering from some kind of psychosomatic disease. They are really ill, but it is connected to their mental hygiene and spiritual hygiene as well as to their body.

So there is more to the world than anyone even guessed twenty years ago. But God knows it all. He gives insight into it through revelation in the Bible.

The Bible is not a textbook on sex. It primarily teaches us about ourselves. First, it says we're his creation. Second, we're persons with real value. Third, God loves us and wants us to achieve the highest possible good. He wants the best for us. Then he gives us insights, certain suggestions, that help us realize those things. They include some statements about sex.

If a non-Christian says, "That's just arbitrary; that's what Christians believe," they're right. Don't argue with them. It is "just what Christians believe." There's nothing obvious about the Christian view being right. If it were obvious, it wouldn't need revelation.

You don't wear out your organs through sex. On the surface things can go along just fine. But there's more to life than what goes on at the surface. That's why Christians believe we need insights from beneath the surface, where only God can see. So when we read in the Bible, "flee fornication," we do.

You can call that mindless repression if you want to. I prefer to call it maturity.

When I was a kid I made a napkin holder for my mom. I wanted to complete it in one day. It came time to paint it, and I kept touching it to see if it was dry. My mom still has that napkin holder, finger marks and all. She keeps it on the table to remind her that I was once a boy. But it reminds me of immaturity. Immaturity means I couldn't wait.

That's the way it is with sex. It's hard to put it off. Let's not kid around about that. But that's what needs to be done. And learning how to do it is a way of learning how to be mature. It pays off in the mature love—in marriage, the intimate world I described earlier, which really is "going all the way."

And who wants to get impatient and miss that?

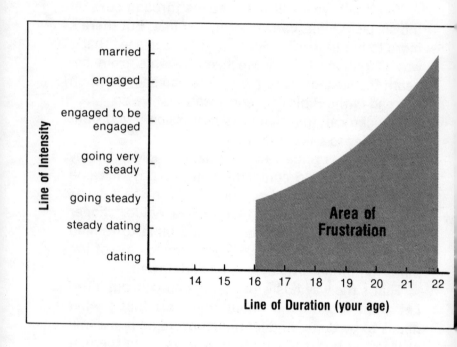

10

spread the word

I became a Christian while I was in high school. It was like fireworks going off in my life. Overnight I felt different. I acted differently.

I guess I followed a typical pattern. I learned from other Christians that I was supposed to witness, to tell people about Jesus. And I went at it whole-heartedly. I went around telling everybody they needed to be saved. If I went somewhere and failed to tell somebody about their eternal destiny, I'd feel guilty.

You don't have to be a genius to figure out what happened. People were turned off. Pretty soon they didn't want to talk with me. They weren't inviting me to parties, and they weren't enthusiastic about spending time with me. Even my family was alien-ated.

Of course, I thought this was proof of how pure I was: "What have the children of light to do with the children of darkness?" I told myself they were rejecting God, not me. And I kept on busily talking to everybody I could buttonhole.

It was years later that I woke up. I realized that I'd erected barriers between myself and former friends. I couldn't talk about anything but religion. I'd become a self-centered fanatic. I thought people were rejecting God, while actually they weren't closed at all to Christ. They just didn't want to become weird like me.

That's when I went back and began rebuilding the bridges I'd destroyed. I'd had no time to simply be **friends** with those people. I'd been too busy witnessing to be interested in things they were interested in. I'd had no time to laugh, cry, celebrate with them. Consequently, they wouldn't listen to me. It's only fair, really. I wasn't listening to them, why should they listen to me?

As I rebuilt those bridges, I was also studying the Bible. I noticed a very interesting thing there about the word "witness." For me, to "witness" was to get some tracts and go out and talk to people. It was something I did. But the Bible didn't use "witness" that way very much. "Witness" was a noun much more often than it was a verb. A "witness" was a person who had Jesus Christ in his life.

Gradually it dawned on me. I didn't have to go out on the streets and preach to be a witness. I **was** a witness. I didn't have any choice in the matter. The day I accepted Jesus Christ into my life, I became a witness. People could look at me and say, "So that's what God does to people."

That changed everything. You see, I had the idea that you heard a sermon and got charged up, and then you went out and gave this spiel. If you were a good speaker, could think clearly, and knew the right techniques, then you were a "good witness."

But witnessing isn't what you do, it's what you are. So what is a "good" witness? A good witness must be roughly the same as a good person, measured by Christ's standards. A good witness is somebody you want to be with. A good witness is somebody whose style of life shows that Christ is having an effect on his life. He shows it not only in what he says, but in what he does.

my new car

I remember the first time I ever owned a brand-new car. I was proud. I couldn't wait for my wife to send me to the store for a quart of milk so I could show it off. I'd drive slowly past friends' houses, wave to people—I wanted everyone to see I had a new car.

A good witness has that kind of natural enthusiasm. You don't worry so much about how and when to say things as much as **being.** You concentrate on Jesus Christ. Then when you talk, you're sharing the joy and love you've found—not some packaged message that belongs to someone else.

There's a beautiful example of that kind of witness in Acts 3 and 4. Peter and John were on their way to the temple, and they healed a lame beggar on the way. It caused quite a stir which ended when

Peter and John were arrested and forbidden by the authorities to spread their message. Peter and John said, "You decide whether God wants us to obey you instead of him! We cannot stop telling about the wonderful things we saw Jesus do and heard him say."

We can be like them. People might laugh at us for talking about God; they might give us a hard time. But we ignore those reasons. We obey God— and we cannot stop telling about the wonderful things Jesus does and says.

But that means talking about what Jesus means to **you.** If your heart is empty, if your Christian life really doesn't mean much to you, if you don't have any joy or fulfillment in life, don't go trying to give it to other people. But if God **is** doing something in your life, then you'll want to tell about it.

There will be other urges, too—fear and shyness. They'll make you want to be quiet. But there will be the basic urge to share something good with people you care about. That is the urge you should pay attention to.

holy hammerlock?

Suppose you want to share what God is doing. How do you go about it? Get a hammerlock on every person who comes near you and talk their ear off?

No. Rely on God to work. I used to force my way into situations. Now I know that the Holy Spirit will open doors for me if I ask. Try starting your day by praying, "Please open up some opportunities for me to share my trust in you." You can pray for spe-

cific people this way, too: "Please let some of the
time we spend talking turn to serious things." I've
found that when I do that, God will open things up
in a beautiful way . . . no strain. People will say,
"Boy, I just don't know how it was you who happened my way." But I know. It was the Holy Spirit
going ahead of me.

Just as important as prayer is knowing what your
goals are.

"I know what I want," you say. "I want my friends
to become Christians."

But think that out. All of us tend to want everybody else just like us. We have a cookie-cutter approach. We want everyone molded to the shape we
think a Christian ought to have. If you look closely at
the mold you're using, it usually looks a lot like your
own face.

That approach doesn't even make copies. All it
communicates is, "I'm good and you're bad. I'm going to heaven and you're going to hell. I'm an in-
sider; you're an outsider." That doesn't excite
people about Jesus. Nobody wants to be treated like
a welfare case.

You have to build bridges to other people in order
to communicate. The good news about Jesus is a
heavy message: it takes a strong bridge. The strong-
est bridge is what I call an "I care" bridge. "I care
about you as a person," it says. "I'm not telling you
this just to get another notch in my belt."

"you're going to hell"

How do you build that kind of bridge? One thing's

for sure, you can't pretend you're interested in someone just so you can get your message across. They'll spot you as a phony sooner or later. No, if you don't care about other people as persons—not targets—you'd better start praying God will make you care about them. He's the only one who can.

After that, building bridges is just like building any friendship. You listen to others. You show an interest in what they care about. You show flexibility by doing what they want some of the time.

I know of a girl who went to her Campus Life club director and said she'd tried everything to win her school to Christ, and they were just laughing at her. So he asked her what she'd done.

"Well," she said, "I go early every day and put tracts in lockers telling the kids they're going to hell. Then at noon hour, I take my Bible and stand in back of the school. I preach to them and tell them they're lost."

The club director made her promise to stop preaching and putting tracts in their lockers. He said, "Just try an experiment. Do you know of any one person you'd particularly like to reach?"

She thought about it. There was one girl she was particularly concerned about.

"Well, what does she like to do?" he asked.

"She likes to swim, I guess. She goes to the YMCA a lot."

So he told her to start swimming with her.

"But I don't like to swim," she said.

"Well," he said, "maybe she doesn't like to be a Christian."

So the girl began to go to the Y with her. She went for five or six weeks, and nothing happened. Finally one day the girl turned to her and said, "Why are you doing this?"

Then she told her she liked her and thought she was a fine person, and she shared her faith. For the first time the girl was really interested in hearing it. She said, "I used to think you were weird. Now I can see you're a real person!"

That's the kind of attitude you want to communicate. You don't want to say, "Become exactly like me." It's more, "We're both beggars going hungry, and I've found out where they give out food. I want to share it."

the big hurt

I was in a church in Chicago a few years ago, and when I was leaving I walked out to my car and found a man leaning against it. He asked me if I had a minute.

He said, "I want to share something with you, Jay. Tell me why this is: I've been in this church thirty years. I've been a deacon; I've gone door-to-door talking to people; I've done just about everything. And all these years I've never really led anyone to Christ."

He went on to tell me that last year his son had gotten into trouble. He had raped a girl in the neighborhood. It got into the papers. Everybody knew about it. He and his wife were ashamed to go to church, ashamed even to go out of their house. Finally they decided they couldn't hide from the world forever, so they started back to church.

"Do you know what's happened?" he said. "In the last year at least half a dozen men have come to me in private, told me their deepest problems, and asked me for help. I've had more chances to talk to people in one year than I had in thirty. Now why is that?"

"Why do you think it is?" I said.

"Maybe," he said, "it's because people want help from someone they know needed help of his own. Maybe they feel that because you have been hurt you'll understand them when they are hurt." He thought a little more, and said, "You know, Jay, it was an awful thing to have happen, and I'd never want it to happen again. But maybe it had to happen so I could learn this lesson. People put up a front trying to appear perfect, and they're cutting themselves off from the chance they have to help other people."

Ask yourself, "What kind of help are people looking for?" For instance, if you get a D on a test, who do you look for—a kid with an A? Or do you look around for a kid with a D or an F? You probably find the other kid who failed and go commiserate over a Coke with him.

The world is not waiting for the perfect Christian with all the answers to ride in on his white horse and say, "Be like me." People are looking for someone who has problems like they have but is working them out. A person who honestly says he has faith in

Christ but admits he's facing difficulties, who says
he doesn't have all the answers, will communicate.
He'll communicate as a real human being. Only ro-
bots don't have problems. Just testify up to the
level of your own faith. Don't try to put on a faith
bigger than what you have. Be honest. Don't chicken
out and say less than you believe, but don't pretend
and say **more** than you honestly can.

as intimate as bad breath

Though our society is a lot more liberated in some
ways than it was a few decades ago, there are some
things considered as bad as ever. One of the worst
things you can imagine is somebody going up to a
stranger and saying, "You have bad breath."

But sometimes we want to tell people that.

So there is an ad on TV which suggests a more
subtle way of telling them. You leave a bottle of
Scope sitting around.

Well, if breath is that intimate, I would say the
soul is at least equally intimate. If you're going to
talk to someone about his soul, you surely are going
to be as tactful as you would be talking to him about
his breath. There you're just talking about social
disgrace. Here you're talking about eternal disgrace.

Choosing an appropriate time to speak is part of
this. Do you go at someone when he's in a group of
people? Not if you're smart. Few people are willing
to talk about intimate things when friends are standing around threatening their self-esteem.

The same is true of arguing. People aren't usually

open to changing their minds when they might lose face. If you disagree with a teacher, you don't have to start arguing in class. Come around later and say, "I appreciate what you said, but I've thought about it this way." It's just common sense that you'll get farther by being polite. Avoid putting the other person in an awkward spot.

And make sure what you claim to be faith isn't fear in disguise. Are you afraid of what the other person has to say? Afraid of the weakness of your own position? It always shows through as defensive, and it undermines what you say. Some people have the attitude, "When you're unsure, yell louder." But that doesn't communicate. The only person who can afford to be quiet and calm is the person who is confident in his beliefs.

guerrilla tactics

A good witness is never worried about being in the minority. In fact, he knows he's in trouble the minute he gets a majority consensus.

The New Testament idea is that one individual is like yeast in the dough. A little bit goes a long way toward permeating everything around it.

The Christian is called to be that little bit of yeast. He knows he's in the minority, but it doesn't bother him. He believes he has truth on his side, and he inserts truth in situations and lets it grow and cause things to happen. He speaks out against racism, against hatred, against lust, not just by what he says but by the way he acts. By doing that he becomes a good witness. A person who knows him is an eyewitness to what God does.

These are minority tactics. The New Testament doesn't teach people how to run things, or how to violently overthrow the rotten system. It teaches quiet people how to move into others' lives and plant powerful ideas in their minds. When you go into a school, you don't expect everything to be just the way you want it. That doesn't mean you go around eating martyr pills all the time, giving people reasons to hate you. But it does mean certain things will never be popular on this earth, and we shouldn't expect them to be.

I own a book that lists the ten rules Ho Chi Minh had for his soldiers in Vietnam. They're very simple rules: things like, when you go into a house, take off your shoes; never kill a chicken inside the house; never touch a woman. They stress politeness more than military strength. It doesn't sound like a powerful strategy. But it won over more villages than huge tanks did. The tank seemed powerful, but what was happening behind the scenes was different. The whole philosophy of guerrilla warfare is based on getting inside people's heads, not overpowering them.

By that standard, the Bible is a manual for guerrilla warfare. There are instructions like "Love your enemy; do good to those who despise you and use you. Turn the other cheek; walk the second mile." Those are minority tactics. They catch people off guard. They speak louder than words.

You see, fanaticism is never too much Christ—
it's too little brains. How can you have too much
Christ? How could you possibly be too loving, gentle,
kind, forgiving?

help, I'm a failure!

When I became a Christian I got the idea that if
everybody I knew didn't become a Christian, I must
be some kind of failure. I ran around like crazy doing
everything I could, and then doing some more. And
I still felt it wasn't enough.

It didn't occur to me that by my standards Jesus
Christ was a failure. Most of the people he contacted
never put their faith in him. Eventually I realized I
didn't have to do anything. God couldn't have
planned so poorly as to leave winning the whole
world up to me! He has lots of ways of reaching a
person. I was acting like I was all God had going for
him.

Christ himself limited his work. He didn't draw on
some superhuman strength so he could preach
day and night. He limited himself to relatively short
times. There were no all-night meetings. He got into
boats to avoid the crowd. You don't see Christ chas-
ing people down, buttonholing them, pushing them
down with one knee on their throat to force his message down.

He didn't act like that because he trusted his
Father to work on those people. He trusted his Father to show him the things that really needed doing.
He believed that his Father wanted to give rest, not
exhaustion. We should be the same way.

can openers

I've mentioned how to ask God to prepare situations for sharing Christ, and how to build bridges of caring to people. I've suggested you ought to share what's happened to you, and be honest in what you say.

But I haven't said a word about the can openers.

Can openers are the little booklets, tracts, or outlines you memorize and use when you witness. They are very helpful. "The Four Spiritual Laws" is one little booklet that is popular. There are others. "The Roman Road," a series of verses in Romans that clearly spells out the message of God's salvation, is another. I don't particularly recommend any one over another, but I do recommend you find one you're comfortable with, and learn it. You might think it'll restrict you, but my experience is that it frees you. It keeps you from talking about a lot of irrelevant stuff when you share your faith and makes sure you remember the crucial data.

But I will offer one word of caution. To hear some people, can openers **are** evangelism. They're not. The witness to Christ is you. No gimmick can do it for you.

But it can help. That's why I call them can openers. They help open the subject. They sometimes get you past the awkwardness. They bring the crucial stuff out into the open so you can talk about it.

If you want to know more about the specifics, I'd suggest you read Paul Little's book **How to Give Away Your Faith.**

Most of all, I'd stress the point I started with. A witness is a noun before it is a verb. It is what you are more than what you do. If you are living in Christ, you are a witness to him. If you are learning and growing in him, it will show in the kind of person you become. It won't matter whether you're a forceful speaker, whether you're shy or meet people easily. Your character will speak to people in what you say and in what you do. All through your life, in thousands of ways, people will learn about Jesus Christ because of what you are. That's what Jesus wants from you.

Further reading from WORD BOOKS—

BEYOND THE GOAL. By Kyle Rote, Jr., with Ronald Patterson. The inside story of a genuine, home-grown, 100 percent American superstar, Kyle Rote, Jr.: winner of ABC's 1974 and 1976 Superstars competition; star striker for the Dallas Tornado pro soccer team; unabashed Christian man's man with a big, generous heart. #80390.

GOD GOES TO HIGH SCHOOL. By James Hefley. Story of the Youth For Christ movement from its early days of mass appeal to its current individual and personal outreach, together with a glimpse of the exciting future of the movement as it spreads world-wide. #90014 (mass paperback).

MY BROTHER DENNIS. By Dennis Benson. Is there a way for you to be significant in the lives of others at their moments of change, reflection, and crisis? Dennis Benson is not an "answer kind of person." But, as he relates "a debriefing of my heart and mind," you will discover key clues to your own human giving. A moving witness to a unique style of caring. #80367.

I BELIEVE. By Grant Teaff with Sam Blair. The dramatically successful Baylor University football coach talks about his life and faith. "I don't care how many championships you win or how successful you are or how much money you make, you're the biggest loser who ever came down the pike if God is not in the center of your life." #80411.

THROUGH IT ALL. By Andraé Crouch with Nina Ball. The story of a man who makes music people love. Here is Andrae's conversion and the amazing account of how he received God's gift of music. Composer, arranger, pianist, and soloist, Andrae Crouch has gained international recognition performing with the group he formed in 1956—"America's Number One Soul Gospel Group," Andrae Crouch and The Disciples. #80370; #98029 (quality paperback).

IF MY PEOPLE . . . A Handbook for National Intercession. By Jimmy and Carol Owens. Jimmy and Carol Owens believe that the Scriptures reveal God's requirements for the healing of our nation—and for the people of God, His church, as His holy nation. This talented couple have shared their convictions in a new musical. In this handbook, they share the call to National Intercession in the greater depth of the printed word. #98034 (quality paperback); #91000 (Leader's Guide); #91001 (Response Manual).

GOD IS A VERB. By Marilee Zdenek and Marge Champion. Here are refreshing winds of change to renew your spirit, captured in prayer poems by Marilee and action photos by Marge. You'll find dragons to be faced, frogs to be kissed. You'll laugh and celebrate. #80306.

CATCH THE NEW WIND. By Marilee Zdenek and Marge Champion. Combines every element—drama, art, Scripture, liturgy, music, lighting, and literature—along with detailed information about the properties and production techniques necessary—into an indispensable handbook for creative worship. "A much-needed book"—Catherine Marshall. #80272.

THE GUTTER AND THE GHETTO. By Don Wilkerson with Herm Weiskopf. Dave Wilkerson told about the beginning of Teen Challenge's work among troubled teenagers in New York City. Now his brother Don, Director of Teen Challenge, brings you up to date on the amazing growth of this ministry. #90012 (mass paperback).